Making Our Home Across the Seas

Making Our Home Across the Seas

Stories from a Captain and a Nurse

Translated and Edited By
David Ho and Peter T. Ho

WHITECAPS
PRESS

Boston

PUBLISHED BY WHITECAPS PRESS

Copyright © 2020 by Peter T. Ho
All rights reserved. This book or any portion thereof
may not be reproduced, duplicated, transmitted or
used in any manner whatsoever in either
electronic means or printed format without the
expressed written permission of the publisher except for
the use of brief quotations in a book review.
Recording of this publication is strictly prohibited.

Cover design by Melissa Gattuso
Proofreading by Brooks Becker

Printed in the United States of America

First printing July 2020

Print ISBN: 978-1-7349385-4-8

Library of Congress Control Number: 2020909942

For our parents, Henry Y.H. Ho (何毓衡)
and Peggy S. Ho (何薛真培)

Without them, the events in their lives,
apart and together, would never have occurred
to be chronicled in their original Chinese essays.
Without their stories, we would not have understood
that our home can be anywhere across the seas
where we and our loved ones are willing to venture.
Without their writings, this book of translations of just
some of their published works could not have been.
And, of course, without them,
we could not have been.

Contents

Foreword ix
England: 1945 to 1948 1
   1. From India to England 3
   2. How We Learn New Skills 13
   3. Hut Number 9 and Pamela 23
   4. A Story of Seeing a Ghost 35
   5. War of the Roses 45
   6. *Chang Feng* for Ten Thousand Miles ["長風"萬里] 55
China: 1949 65
   7. Game of Checkers in Life 67
   8. A Life of a Postman 77
Taiwan: 1950 to 1964 89
   9. A Gunnery Petty Officer and His Trumpet 91
  10. Holy Water 97
  11. *The Story of The New York Times, 1851-1951* 109
United States: 1965 to 1988 117
  12. Repressed Tears of Chinese Students in America 119
  13. I Am a Nurse 127
  14. A Chinese Family in America 135
  15. From Captain to Bricklayer 141
Fiction 149
  16. Comedy on the Whitecaps 151
  17. Typhoon Night 163

Remembrances 177
18. Henry Ho 179
19. Peggy Ho 183
Original Chinese Articles 189
20. Game of Checkers in Life..191
21. A Life of a Postman..195
22. Holy Water 199
23. A Chinese Family in America 205
Major Works of Henry and Peggy Ho..207
About the Translators 211

Foreword

It may be clichéd to say that your father is your hero, but he really was mine.

Ever since I was a child, I have always thought that if I could grow up to be half the man our father was, I would be a success. Now that David and I have worked to translate this collection of representative articles from his countless published works into this book, I can begin to say that I am in the process of becoming half the man that he was.

Our father, Henry Ho, was a prolific author and translator. While writing was not his profession, it was much more than a hobby. Over the course of his life, he wrote countless original essays and fictional short stories in Taiwan-based and Hong Kong-based magazines and newspapers, authored his own books, and translated many others from English to Chinese. He encouraged our mother to write original pieces and to translate books as well.

One overriding observation about our father, endorsed by everyone who knew him, is that he loved children – all children, those in his immediate and extended family as well as any others who happened to traverse into his orbit. When I was growing up in suburban New Jersey, we frequently attended weekend dinner parties with other immigrant Chinese families in the area. If my father was not sitting with his friends, he would invariably be found rolling on the ground while surrounded by laughing toddlers and young children who would be climbing over him.

He passed away at age sixty-five when his first two grandchildren, David's daughters, were four and six. He would never meet his other two grandchildren, my sons, who were born after his death. My biggest regret is that except for Clara, his oldest grandchild, his grandchildren did not get to know him. His four grandchildren, Clara, Candace, Andrew, and Brian, would have been the apples of his eye, and he would have spoiled them silly. Although our mother lived to eighty-two and lived to see both granddaughters graduate college and both grandsons enter high school, she and our father, like many members of the Greatest Generation, spoke little of their past and their life events. As a result, David and I knew only a few tidbits about the many adventures they experienced in England, China, and Taiwan. And their grandchildren know even less than we do.

David and I originally started the Chinese to English translation of a representative sampling of our father's and mother's published works in Chinese as a way to acquaint our children with the grandparents whom they either never met or barely remember. We wanted to use their own words to tell about their marriage together, their life experiences, and their keen observation skills, but mostly their appreciation of the lives they were given. We wanted to pass these stories on to our children, to other members of their extended family – especially those from the most recent generation, what would be their great-grandchildren – and to those outside our circle of family and friends who never had the opportunity to know Henry and Peggy Ho.

Whether this is the sole collection of English translations of their writings or just the first of many volumes to come, we hope that the perspectives they conveyed about the breadth of historical events that they lived through, including World War II, the Chinese Civil War, the Nationalist evacuation to Taiwan, and immigration to the United States during President Johnson's Great Society, prove insightful and engaging to all readers, not just those in our family. In retrospect, it is clear to us now that their struggles and perseverance through this sequence of modern historical events, like beads on a string, served a higher purpose: to search for better education and life opportunities for us, their children.

As you read through this small sampling of our parents' published works, whether in the original Chinese or our translations, it should be clear that they both enjoyed the written word. Our father completed English-to-Chinese translations of at least eleven books that we know of

Foreword

and authored two original books of his own, as well as countless essays, commentaries, and fictional short stories over a span of four decades. For him writing was more than a pleasurable diversion; his writing supplemented his relatively limited income as a young naval officer in Taiwan. David can remember our father writing late into the night in our small living room in Taipei that was crammed full of books and papers. After we moved to the United States, writing became less of a means of additional compensation and more of a way to convey the novelty of life in his newly adopted country to those back in Asia who had not yet had the chance to experience the West. Our mother did not sit idly by while our father wrote. She helped to proofread his translations of the many books that he took on. In addition, she published two Chinese translations of whole books and co-authored with him many articles that detailed their worldwide travels during their retirement years.

Our father's English-to-Chinese translation activity was not only an avocation involving works of literature but also a second job that brought in income. He maintained a home-based small business whereby he translated test questions from merchant marine examinations from English to Chinese. The twist of fate that we, his sons, are now translating his and our mother's original publications from Chinese to English is not lost upon us.

We had occasion to share a few of the original Chinese publications with family members as we worked on these translations. Their reflections as they read the pieces written decades ago are provided below:

Evelyn Tong (niece of Henry and Peggy Ho) in October 2019:

> "When I was growing up in Japan, my mom and I visited our Gong-Gong [公公] and Ching-Po [親婆] [Evelyn's paternal grandparents] in Taiwan a few times during the summer. Since I don't have any friends there, I spent a lot of time reading books and magazines Gong-Gong kept in his office/library. I wasn't all that interested in his Postal magazines, but I remember reading many articles your dad wrote in a magazine called *Travelling Magazine* [旅行雜誌]. He wrote about the many places he visited, the people, the sights, the culture, which I found fascinating because my world was limited to Yokohama and Taipei. These articles really opened my eyes and made me dream about traveling to these places someday . . . I guess your dad was a very popular 'travel blogger' in today's world."

Indeed, their writings about their travels to and experiences in different lands would make them prolific "bloggers" in today's world, except they were doing this in the days before the internet and social media.

From Min-Yu Hsueh (nephew of Henry and Peggy Ho) in January 2020:

> "I started reading Uncle's stories. As usual, his stories can absorb me into his world for hours. As a child, I was lucky to be at his side from time to time. Today I am reliving that nearness. I also wonder how Uncle joined the Navy (from his land-locked provincial home) and then became a chosen young officer to train with the British Navy. Too bad I never thought about asking him that question. But what he did affected so many lives positively including mine."

We hope readers will bear in mind that many of the articles were written decades ago, when the world was much different than it is today. What might have been perfectly acceptable and consistent with the thinking and mores of that time may be viewed somewhat differently today. As well, many of our parents' writings were directed at an audience in Taiwan and Hong Kong at a time in their respective histories when the Bamboo Curtain separated parents from children and siblings from one another, and political and ideological tensions between China and Taiwan were manifested as military conflicts in the Taiwan Strait. As translators, we tried to remain true to their words even if they might provoke a different response today. For that, we ask for the reader's indulgence.

Spanning five decades, our parents' writings are a treasure trove that bears witness to their perseverance, survival, and humor as they find love and raise a family in rapidly changing post-war China, Taiwan, and America. At a time when the value of immigration in the United States is under question, even assault, their stories are a relevant reminder of the wealth of perspective, experience, and commitment that immigrants bring to America and the breadth of opportunities that America affords to immigrants who willingly sacrifice the lives they have nurtured in the old country to adopt the United States as their own.

We gratefully acknowledge the support from many as we worked on and off on this project over the past ten years. Our family was our primary source of encouragement and advice, with special thanks to our wives, Lisa and Hui Ping; David's daughters, Clara and Candace; and our cousin Evelyn Tong. Sheng Cui and Ed Zhang provided feedback on the original

Chinese pieces and motivation to continue our work. Melissa Gattuso was invaluable in her guidance on digital imaging and the publishing process. We thank Kelvin Hong for sharing rare historical documents and material regarding the *Chang Feng* group of the SS Chongqing directly and through his website *Glimpses of Modern China* (秋海棠民國史地).

Finally, although David completed most of the heavy lifting of Chinese to English translation, we had the help of two young translators, Enoch Ha and Emrie Tomaiko, along the way.

Peter T. Ho

England: 1945 to 1948

1

From India to England

by Henry Yu-Heng Ho
from *Ship Transfer Commemorative Issue*, 1948

Translators' Note: One of two essays by Henry Ho in tandem with "How We Learn New Skills." From 1945 to 1948, 587 Chinese naval seamen were sent to the United Kingdom for training to take command of the light cruiser HMS Aurora (recommissioned by the Chinese Navy as the SS Chongqing, 重慶艦) and destroyer HMS Mendip (recommissioned as the SS Lin Fu, 靈甫艦). Twenty-nine seamen were promoted to Petty Officer. Our father, Petty Officer First Class Ho, age twenty-five at the time, received specialist training in naval artillery maintenance and repair while in the U.K. At 6,000 tons, the SS Chongqing carried three twin-mounted six-inch guns and was the largest naval warship in the Chinese Navy until the 1990s.

This essay described the seamen's journey from China to England, which for most of them was their first trip to foreign lands.

*****

Across India

On a November evening in 1945, the airplane that brought us south from China had completed its long journey and, with the help of runway lights, we landed safely during the night at Calcutta's Dum Dum Airport. We could immediately sense a tension in the air from the pervasive religious frictions that we had heard about.

Photo: Departing China for Calcutta, November 1945. Original caption reads, "Flying high on the wings of a Chinese transport plane."

We spent the next three days in transit in Calcutta and waited for the train to take us across India. Our first impression of this city was that she was a big and noisy city full of soldiers, sacred cows, and black crows. In short, it was a big, chaotic mess, just like the local bazaars that sprang up at home on the first and fifteenth of each month.

Trains crossing the Indian subcontinent were busy transporting soldiers proudly returning to their homes. We, on the other hand, were traveling with trepidation away from our homes to a foreign land that was still very far away. However, just like those returning soldiers, we were all happy and excited.

The tropical plains of India unfolded before our eyes along the railroad tracks. Unlike at home, there was no autumn foliage covering rolling hills, nor did we see any relaxed post-harvest gatherings on the farms. Instead, we could only see dried grasslands dotted with poorly fed white cows and old and young farmers sitting in front of small broken huts. They looked tired under the scorching sun, which had already darkened their skin. Farmlands were not tilled or planted; the land looked empty and lonely. Men and cows looked lifeless with blank expressions, as if they were lazy or the devil had stolen their souls.

Our train continued to gallop across the plains. At times we stopped to take on water, coal, or food. Military trains had no civilian passengers. Instead, half-naked child beggars routinely appeared at our windows. They uttered some incomprehensible sentences and stuck their hands through the train windows. The smarter ones would stick out a thumb and chant "China ding hao" in an effort to gain more handouts from us. A map helped us to identify the passing stations. After a journey of three days and two nights, we arrived at Bombay, which is located on the western side of India.
(Translators' Note: "China ding hao" is translated as "China is the best.")

Bombay – Memorable Days

The Royal Navy's gray truck took us from the noisy train station through downtown and out along Bombay's luxurious but quieter seaside drive. The beach with its tourist boardwalk and light-green ocean was on one side of the road, while handsome, neatly arranged buildings sat on the other. The streets were dotted with the latest-model cars, and evergreen-covered walls surrounded many villas of the wealthy or residences of government officials. At the end of a row of villas, our truck turned off onto a side road. It stopped in front of another luxurious stone building. Fellow cadets who had arrived earlier greeted us from their balconies. The feeling was of novelty, bewilderment, and fulfillment. We entered this resort hotel and started our memorable days in Bombay.

Photo: Bombay's seaside drive

Perhaps it was the comfortable life and pleasant weather. All of us were left with wonderful memories of Bombay. This resort hotel, appropriated by the Royal Navy, had three of us sharing one room with our own balcony facing the sea. If not for the steel-framed military cots in our room, we could have been living like wealthy tourists on a leisurely vacation.

The winter months on the coast of the Arabian Sea required only a short-sleeve shirt. We were all nervous about passing the Royal Navy's entrance examinations. Two British officers conducted daily English lessons intended to improve our listening and speaking skills. A lame-footed petty officer helped us with marching drills. It took us a while to get used to the highly stylized marching steps, which we thought projected arrogance. However, with greater attention to mimicry, we eventually mastered the unique marching style.

Photo: Marching drills led by British officers. Original caption reads, "Our first taste of a British-style marching drill."

    As it turned out, the examination itself proved to be easier than we had thought. Unfortunately, twenty-six of our comrades were repatriated as they tested positive for tuberculosis. This proved to be a small tragedy during a journey abroad. Sadly, we had to bid them farewell in a foreign land. Carrying local medicines and gifts bought by us for our families in China, they departed with our blessings and sympathies.

    Although Western meals were more nutritious, they sometimes tasted like wax. The local Chinese restaurants became our only joy and salvation. To many of us from China's interior provinces, their lobster and sea cucumber dishes were a new experience. We savored these dishes that left us with a sense of longing for our homes. This contrasted with the filth and prostitution we observed near Bombay's Chinatown, which gave us an initial understanding of the life of overseas Chinese.

Photo: Dining on bland western meals in Bombay

The Christmas we knew from greeting cards and books should be celebrated within a snow-covered landscape with a portly red-suited Santa Claus graciously presenting gifts. However, Christmas for us that year was spent on the beaches of the Arabian Sea, swimming and eating bananas underneath the shade of coconut trees. Occasionally, we were educated by Christians with more details about the holiday. After the New Year, the British authorities booked us on a ship to England. Ironically, we so-called Navy sailors took our first trip at sea like any other ordinary passenger.

Westward

The RMS Empress of Australia was a German ocean liner seized by Britain as a spoil of war during World War I. After this war she was assigned to ferry Allied soldiers back to England. It seemed strange that we took our first sea voyage as passengers. The sea was still new to us, and so were ships. Our eighteen-day ocean passage provided us some idea about what a sailor's life would be like. We sailed through the Arabian Sea, the Red Sea, and the Mediterranean Sea. They all behaved like a gentle girl. After rounding Gibraltar, the Bay of Biscay off of France showed us for the first time the ugly side of the sea. She gave us high winds, giant waves, and heavy fog. With a mariner's career ahead of us, we learned to be patient and to fight seasickness.

Photo: Original caption reads, "Westward to a new life on board of RMS Empress of Australia."

Upon our arrival to England we did not go onshore right away. On a bone-chilling February morning we wrapped ourselves in thick winter clothes against the howling, frigid wind and stepped onto Liverpool. The gray winter sky and the city's seemingly monotonous skyline presented us with a poor first impression. "This is the English weather!" a fellow Army passenger explained as he returned from the tropics.

Photo: Assembling below the bridge of the RMS Empress of Australia

Photo: Original caption reads, "Arrival to foreign land - First steps onto England at Liverpool."

The train to Plymouth was already waiting for us at the station. Post-war England had many war scars remaining from the terrible bombings it received. However, there were also new towns and villages being built, which we greatly admired. Near midnight our train arrived at the Devonport Naval Base. We were immediately ferried onto the training battleship HMS Renown. As we looked around the harbor, huge warships around us were silhouetted against the dark midnight sky. The call of the Navy still seemed quite remote to us.

Our first impression of this warship was to ask how we could live in such narrow spaces below deck. As we touched and felt our way up to the open deck, we came across the giant fifteen-inch double-barreled twin-mounted main gun. Its long barrels lay quietly in the dark amongst all kinds of machines, cables, and weapons that we had never seen.

Sleeping in a hammock for the first time, and with daybreak coming, I was kept awake by my excitement even though my body badly needed rest. I asked my bunkmate how he felt.

"Oh, I don't know, and I am wide awake like you. Ah, the Navy . . ." he sighed.

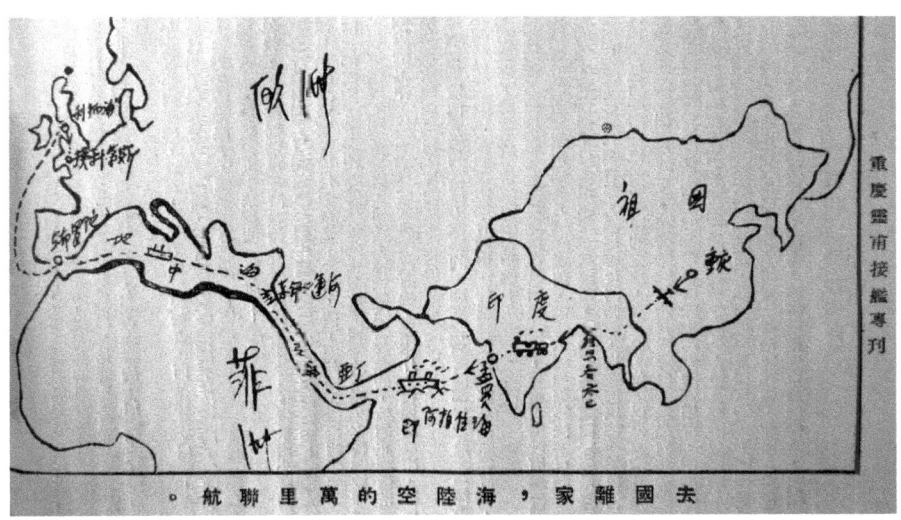

Photo: Hand-drawn map of the crew's journey from Chongqing to Calcutta to Bombay through the Arabian Gulf, Suez Canal, Mediterranean Sea, and Straits of Gibraltar to Liverpool, England (November 1945 to February 1946)

2

How We Learn New Skills
A Journal from the Gunnery Repair Team

by Henry Yu-Heng Ho
from *Ship Transfer Commemorative Issue*, 1948

Translators' Note: One of two essays written by Henry Ho in tandem with "From India to England." This and the first chapter are translated from the original essays printed in 1948 in a book titled Ship Transfer Commemorative Issue (重慶靈甫接艦專刊). *This article describes how the gunnery repair team learned the skills of naval artillery maintenance and repair, which represented an advanced technology and skill not available in China at the time.*

*****

Spring in England came late in April of 1946 as we completed basic training on the HMS Renown. Upon returning from our first extended shore leave, most of the trainees packed our duffle bags and headed out for specialist training elsewhere. The huge battle cruiser now appeared empty and lonely except for the twenty-four of us who remained on board for gunnery and electrical machinery training. Our hope of ever getting off this ship looked dim, and our resentment for her increased. For the time being, it appeared that our next destination would never come. Lieutenant Commander Bingham explained that our team would be enrolled in a six-month machinist training course at the Mechanics Training Establishment Center at a nearby shipyard. Because of its proximity, HMS Renown would regrettably remain as our home. Despite our ill feelings toward this old battle cruiser, the new and exciting surroundings and classes would soon erase our disappointment.

Photo: Mechanics Training Establishment Center

On a typical English morning with neither a lively nor dead grayish sky, we were ferried from HMS Renown to the training center. There, a tall but ordinary-looking naval chief petty officer greeted us. He was a fifties-ish man whose work overalls were wrapped tightly around a large belly and whose pair of rosy cheeks made him look as if he had just downed several pints of beer. A thirty-year naval veteran who looked solid and exhibited a jovial, almost childish manner, Chief Petty Officer Brandon was a machine-repairing specialist and our instructor for becoming a mechanical fitter.

He led us through a tour of the training center, where everything looked new and strange to us. There were many lathes in the workshop, all powered by belts that then drove shafts and connected to various heads and gears. The whole place looked busy yet exciting; welders-to-be were practicing arc welding with sparks flying off here and there while raging fires burned brightly in iron-smelting furnaces. The thought that we would be learning how to operate each of these machines one by one so we could maintain our own warship excited me. I felt happy and excited yet anxious and rather intimidated by what lay ahead. "Don't be a stranger here," Brandon told us at the end of our tour. He showed us his large palms as he continued. "Kids, your brain may be your master, but your hands are your real assets."

On the next day, we suited up for training. Brandon brought us some hammers and files plus several simple drawings. With a piece of raw iron clamped to a vise, we began our six months of training our "hands" indeed! As we learned how to use these bench tools, we quickly realized how unskilled and reluctant our hands were. To file and shape a piece of irregularly shaped metal using only hand tools was already a difficult task, but producing a piece that met a drawing's dimensional tolerances was a bigger headache. While teaching us tool and die skills, Brandon often said, with a confident and experienced look on his face, "Look, kids, it's easy." We could only then envy his thick, muscular arms while admiring even more what those arms could make.

Manually forging a piece of steel with a hammer is a most troublesome task to master. When we struck each piece mercilessly hard, the mischievous hammer would often bounce back and reverberate painfully in our hands, which became red and swollen. They would bleed as we continued. Although he had gone through the same painful experience, Old Man Brandon still got a kick out of seeing our awkward and pained faces! He would walk over and braggingly demonstrate how to raise the hammer high and still strike it hard with precision. He would then say, "Look, it's easy." A few fellow cadets would reply to him in Chinese, "Of course, easy for you, old man. You've been doing this for twenty or thirty years!" Not knowing what was being said, he would turn around or lean over and ask, "Huh?" His puzzled expression made us laugh, and so we continued with the whacking of metal. After a while, our skills improved and the striking did not hurt our hands. Feeling more confident, we started to imitate Brandon's familiar saying back to him, "Look, it's easy . . ." Old Man Brandon would then give us a nod and a wink, then walk away with hands crossed behind his back while humming his favorite tune, which none of us knew!

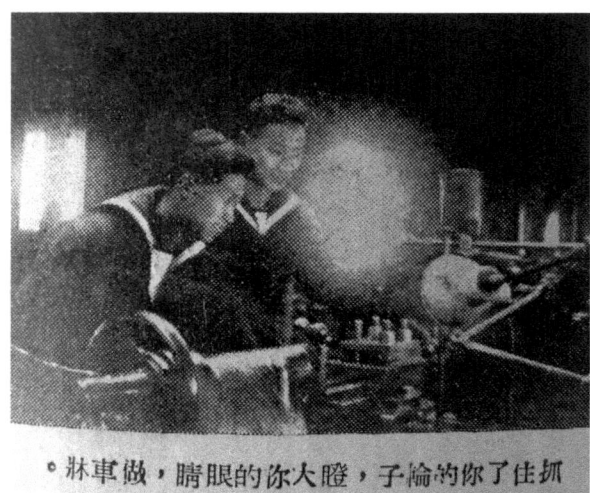

○ 抓住了你的輪子，睜大你的眼睛，做車牀。

Photo: Henry Ho at left. Original caption reads, "Grasping the hand wheel and keeping eyes opened widely, we learn how to operate the lathe."

After three months of hard work under Brandon, our arms thickened and our hands became skillful. A precision tolerance of one to two millimeters no longer scared us. Evening classes were added twice a week with Brandon as our instructor teaching from a machinist's textbook. After we passed our required examinations, we moved on to lathe operation. This was more relaxing and interesting than bench fitting, but we learned we had to be more attentive. Working with a machine tool, we experienced a greater joy of transforming a shapeless piece of raw material into a properly scaled end product. Old Man Brandon was no longer our instructor except for the evening classes since his expertise was mechanical fitting. Occasionally, he would help us with the lathe, but he no longer exhibited the same at-ease expression as we progressed through gas and electric arc welding followed by brass fitting. Soon our six months of training was over. With a tired but happy mindset, we left for annual leave. Even today, I often reminisce about Brandon's introductory remark, "Your hands are your real asset."

At the beginning of 1947, seven of us left the cursed HMS Renown with a great feeling of reprieve! At twilight we arrived at our long-dreamed-of destination – HMS Excellent Gunnery School. The school,

How We Learn New Skills

located on an island in the city of Portsmouth, is also known as the Whale Island Gunnery School. This school has a rich history, is well-equipped, and is known for its strict training discipline, just like the U.S. Military Academy at West Point in America. The school offered training in both gunnery operation and repair. We were assigned to the latter program. At Whale Island our team pledged to work hard while respecting ourselves and others. We finished our studies with good grades and earned the respect of our instructors. To this day, I still reminisce about the great times at Whale Island.

Photo: Henry Ho (second from right) and fellow students build a snowwoman at Whale Island School. Original caption reads, "Fair maiden made of snow, you warm my heart during the cold winter."

Time moved on; spring returned as the flowers blossomed again. We moved on to a new subject, which was the fire control and target calculation systems. We learned about the three components of a gun control tower: gun director, range finder, and calculation table. Advanced technologies were incorporated into these systems to provide our ship with accurate firing solutions. Lieutenant Wood served as our instructor and we are truly thankful for the clarity of his lecturing.

Photo: Henry Ho (leftmost) at mealtime. Original caption reads, "Beer and chicken dinner to rid us of extreme longing for home during the Lunar New Year."

Photo: Henry Ho (second from right) with fellow gunnery repair students at Whale Island

Although studies at Whale Island were intense and demanding, our school was set in beautiful garden-like surroundings full of well-manicured lawns, fragrant flower beds, and winding garden paths. Whale

Island was a wonderful place to study. Its large campus also accommodated fellow naval trainees from India, Egypt, France, and Holland. Many years ago Japan also sent its trainees here from across thousands of miles. The rise and fall of the Empire of the Rising Sun was fated to her navy, a lesson that reminded us of why we were here in England.

After each night's lights-out taps was played, the thick wartime blackout curtains in our dormitory were drawn tightly. Working through the stillness of the night, we busily but quietly reviewed our daytime class notes and diligently copied sketches and drawings from textbooks. It was just like our days as schoolboys; however, this time we worked not just to pass the examinations, but to learn to serve our own warship and country.

Upon completion of our studies at Whale Island, we bid farewell to the school's Commandant. He told us that Lieutenant Parker of HMS Aurora (the maiden name of our own cruiser SS Chongqing) requested our participation in the actual overhauling of HMS Aurora. The Commandant's departing words were, "We are very satisfied and pleased with your progress here, especially in view of the language difficulty. Although you have completed your study here, your real learning will start as you join in Aurora's overhaul."

SS Chongqing (née HMS Aurora) was at dry dock for its post-war overhaul, which included the inspection and repair of all of her weapons. We were the first Chinese Navy personnel to board her before her handover from the Royal Navy. Wearing the same work overalls, we worked side-by-side with our British colleagues. Like coal miners, we often entered the unseen parts of the ship's cavernous interior. We squeezed ourselves into hidden bulkhead voids to disassemble and check every part of the gun turret. The dirty and greasy environment did not dampen but only increased our spirits. The thought that "She will soon be our own warship" was on everyone's mind.

Although we gradually assumed responsibility for the various repairs, there was still much to learn. "You can't fix a gun with your mouth!" was a humorous saying we frequently repeated to each other with some truth to it, much like Petty Officer Brandon's old saying about hands being "our real asset." We hoped that our country will have more and better "brains and hands" to build a strong navy.

Photo: The gunnery and electrical repair team, the first group of Chinese seamen to board the HMS Aurora, in front of her main six-inch guns. Henry Ho is fourth from the right.

As time passes, we will someday grow old, weak, and retire from our beloved seas to return to our birthplace on land. However, the memory of HMS Aurora, forged in our minds by Brandon, and our exciting months spent on Whale Island will remain with us like the fresh memory of yesterday.

Photo: SS Chongqing (formerly HMS Aurora) in Singapore, July 1948

How We Learn New Skills

Photo: SS Chongqing Gunnery Department roster. Henry Ho is listed vertically in the fifth column from the right.

Translation of Henry Ho's roster entry from Chinese:

Rank	Petty Officer First Class
Serial Number	1079
Home Province	Hunan
Age	25
Specialty	Gunnery repair
School	Central Army Logistical School, 17th session

3

Hut Number 9 and Pamela

by Henry Yu-Heng Ho
from his book *Blue Water Memories*, 1964

Translators' Note: Nearly 600 Chinese Navy personnel were shipped to England at the end of World War II to take over the light cruiser HMS Aurora and the destroyer HMS Mendip. They represented hand-picked volunteers from various Chinese military units. Our father volunteered from the Chinese Army Logistic and Supply School at the age of eighteen. After general seamanship training from the Royal Navy, these seamen were assigned specialist trainings based on their test results. Seven were picked to receive comprehensive gunnery training on how to maintain the six-inch main guns. These guns later became the largest naval guns within the Nationalist Chinese Navy.

*****

HMS Excellent

In late 1946, seven of us completed an eight-month mechanics training course at the Royal Navy School in Plymouth. We were next assigned to attend the Whale Island Gunnery School near Portsmouth at Hampshire. Comments made by our training instructor at Plymouth worried us:

> "Whale Island Gunnery School is considered by many as the best naval gunnery school in the world; it is also one of the toughest schools. They tolerate few or no mistakes there! You will find everything at HMS Excellent is excellent and the roads there are made for running but not for walking. Thank heavens I never had to go there. I heard the instructors there are barking dogs."

(Translators' Note: HMS Excellent was the Royal Navy's name for the school. Running was a well-known disciplinary method at Whale Island.)

However, we had stayed at Plymouth too long and were looking for changes. Feeling both excited and fearful, we reported to HMS Excellent in early 1947.

(Translators' Note: Henry Ho received instruction and training at Whale Island in 1947 when he was twenty years old.)

The school was located on an island with a typical picturesque British garden setting. The base was established at a time when one could not distinguish whether Great Britain had a Navy or just had pirates. It was the oldest on-shore training establishment in the Royal Navy where traditions and old buildings were well preserved. Although its barracks were modern inside, their external appearance remained the same as the old days. It was not an exaggeration to describe Whale Island as a beautiful garden. However, it was also not easy to imagine the art of modern weaponry intermixed with the art of gardening.

We were not assigned to a historical building but rather were given a Quonset hut of our own that was located between two old buildings. This hut appeared to be a temporary training facility provided by the Americans during World War II, when many sailors had to be quickly trained. Hut No. 9 became our home and the "Chinese Concession" on Whale Island.

Photo: Whale Island (circa 2017), a man-made island in Portsmouth Harbor, is home to HMS Excellent, the oldest on-shore training establishment within the Royal Navy and the location of the Navy Command Headquarters

During the reception meeting with the base commanding officer (CO), he left us with an interesting thought: "Lads, 90 percent of the British naval staff has been to China. Unfortunately, I belong to the other 10 percent. If I am unable to fulfill my wish to see China someday, you will be the China in my mind."

The Impossible Demonstration

Whale Island Gunnery School also trained other foreigners who were mostly Europeans from countries such as Holland and Denmark. While these nations had no gunnery school of their own, their close ties with Great Britain resulted in their navies having the same ships and weapons as the Royal Navy. Their cadets would arrive at Whale Island in their own warships and proceed directly to the classroom using Royal Navy facilities with their instructors. The school also trained many naval personnel from the French and British colonies.

The Base CO's remark got us thinking, *What can we do to leave him with a good impression of the 'new China'? We should achieve good grades and exhibit good behavior, but these things take time.* So we decided that our top priority was to turn our "Chinese Concession" into a ship-shape showcase at HMS Excellent. In other words, we should pass our barracks inspection with top honors.

We first divided Hut No. 9 into three sections. The front section became our guest and study areas, the middle section was made into sleeping quarters, while the rear became our mess hall. Although such an arrangement did not meet the base regulations, the school tolerated this new configuration. Chief Petty Officer Morgan, assigned to look after Hut No. 9, was a very accommodating person. His slogan was, "What can I do to help you?" He was always willing to assist us.

We next arranged our sleeping quarters in the Whampoa style. All beds and cabinets would be of the same size, color, and shape. To impress our inspectors, we decided that all silverware and our floor would be polished and shined. After receiving our requisition list for cleaning supplies, Mr. Morgan was puzzled.

(Translators' Note: Whampoa Military Academy [黃埔軍校] was China's equivalent of the United States Military Academy at West Point.)

He asked, "Why do you need the floor wax and a waxing machine?"

Xiao Zhou replied, "We want to wax our deck." To us, the deck meant the floor.

"I can understand waxing a wooden floor, but why do you want to wax a cement floor?"

Our request was unusual, and we were short of a good answer. One of our quick-thinking shipmates answered, "We know, but what's the difference?"

"What's the diff--" Morgan stopped and changed the subject. "Do you wax cement floors in China?"

"Yes, sometimes we do." By now, we had established a casual relationship with Morgan.

"Very well, I will get them and I shall look forward to seeing the result."

"You wait and see, Boss." Boss was our affectionate name for Mr. Morgan.

If you have never waxed a cement floor, don't try it! We failed badly in the beginning; wax did not spread evenly on a cold cement floor. Even after we succeeded in waxing a part of the floor, the wax would be absorbed quickly by porous cement floor and dried out. If we applied too much wax, the area would turn into an oily black patch. Oily black patches among grayish-white unwaxed cement floor made our floor look like a chef's greasy apron.

However, we were determined not to fail. After hours of trying, we found the answer!

We first thoroughly washed the cement floor, then we melted and poured a thin layer of wax quickly over the cleaned floor and polished the area while the wax was still warm. Our success came at a price of seven men laboring over many hours plus twenty cans of wax courtesy of the British Empire. We even had to bribe Morgan with beers for extra wax.

Barracks inspection came on Saturday. Early in the morning and before the inspection, Boss Morgan wanted to see the result himself. We jokingly refused him because we wanted to surprise him. We also did not want others to learn and copy our recipe for success.

As part of our preparation, we walked barefoot on the cold floor before the inspection. Driven by our desire to succeed, our barracks cleaning and arrangement details required much more work than that from our academy days in China.

We also starched and ironed all bedspreads and blankets by ourselves. We carefully folded everything with perfect ninety-degree corners using three sets of custom-made wooden boards. We ordered these wooden boards from the outside and secretly brought them in. They were then carefully hidden after usage.

After all of our preparations, we let Boss Morgan in.

His eyes opened widely. Our waxed floor did not surprise him as much as those perfectly folded blankets and sharp bed sheet corners. He walked directly to a bed, looked above and below to find a hidden prop. He found none. He then carefully pressed the blankets with one finger to confirm that they were soft, and again there was no prop underneath. When he removed his finger, the blanket returned to its straight-line shape again.

Morgan turned around and looked at us in amazement. We behaved like a group of proud magicians and told him, "You can measure it with a ruler. They all have the same height, width, and length!"

Morgan kept on nodding and said, "Of course, of course . . ."

At that moment, he would have believed anything we told him.

Suddenly, as if he had forgotten something, he instructed us to get ready as he would be the first to welcome the Base CO to inspect our hut. He left in a hurry as if something very momentous had truly occurred. He also kept on repeating to himself, "I got to tell him . . ."

The Base CO arrived with his usual number of staff to conduct the barracks inspection. The inspection procedure was similar to what we had in China except that they all thought the perfectly made beds and the waxed floor were some kind of miracle.

We stood at perfect attention during inspection. Morgan was now orchestrating the conversation. "Sir, we never thought about doing this before, but waxing the cement floor in China is not an unusual practice," he told the Base CO and acted as if he was very familiar with our work. The CO simply nodded.

"There is nothing underneath and no prop was used." Morgan gently pressed into the blanket to prove his point. The CO and the other Commanders and officers all followed with curiosity.

"Sir, you can measure it with a micrometer, they are all the same size." Morgan had stolen our line and improved our gauge of precision from a "ruler" to a "micrometer."

The CO laughed, and so did others. He turned around and addressed us. "Young men, you did what I thought was impossible. I am proud to have you here. Commander, please record in the morning orders that all barracks petty officers should come and observe Hut No. 9."

After the CO had left, Morgan sneaked back and said, "Make sure you don't mess up the barracks. I will bring others back very soon."

This episode made Hut No. 9 famous. We had many visitors for days, and these visits became a burden. One shipmate complained and suggested that we should request a second set of furniture. One would be for show, while the other would be for our use.

Snow White

After the barracks inspection, Hut No. 9 attracted attention from many passers-by. While watching the passers-by from our window, we had individually discovered and unanimously agreed that we had found a very beautiful peony flower on Whale Island.

Every morning after 0730, groups of two or three female sailors or officers would pass by our front window on their way to work. One of them particularly attracted everyone's attention and liking. She was not tall and had a petite oriental body frame. We took turns to admire her beauty through the window. Ever since Hut No. 9 became famous, she would walk past our hut and throw a deliberate glance at our way over her shoulder.

Hut Number 9 and Pamela

Photo: Womens' Royal Navy Service sailors, known as Wrens, marching on base

Her beauty was beyond that of the famous ancient Chinese beauty Madam Yang Guifei. Although her quick glance came with no smile, we would describe her as beauty beyond all the courtesans in an emperor's court.

(Translators' Note: Yang Guifei was the Emperor's consort during the Tang dynasty and known as one of the Four Beauties of ancient China.)

After several days, we found out her name was Pamela. She worked at the Paymaster's office. All of us developed romantic feelings for her; however, we all learned through the rumor mill that Pamela was a flower meant for regarding, but not to be touched. Locals would generally remind us, "Her? I suggest that you better save your time and heart for someone else . . ."

We had learned that dating in the Western culture can be an "easy-come, easy-go" relationship. This became especially so in England after World War II, when women outnumbered men by many. We also found out that Pamela had no steady boyfriend.

The relationship of admiring her remotely through the window went on and after a while, we became busy with our studies and gradually forgot her.

During our training at Whale Island, the British kept certain critical technologies away from us because we had not earned their trust. This was especially so in the area of fire-control systems. Any materials regarding fire-control directors such as T.S. (Torpedo System) or HACP (High Angle Calculating Position) were only shown to us in the classroom, and no printed copies were made available. We were lucky to understand these advanced topics, let alone try to memorize the details.

This type of learning proved very challenging. Our instructors were sympathetic, but they had to follow orders. Occasionally, they would lend a textbook to us overnight, taking personal liability for doing so. We seized these opportunities whenever they came. We collected our own money and bought graphic tools such as sepia paper to copy drawings and text at night.

We took turns working all night. Our collections started with four-inch guns and moved on to six-inch and eight-inch guns. We even had twelve-inch gun data. However, none of us were iron men, and working at night took its toll. We could barely follow the morning lectures and would easily fall asleep during the afternoon lectures. Our instructors thought we had lost our interest to learn.

(Translators' Note: HMS Aurora, a gift from Britain to China, of which our father and his shipmates would take command in 1948, had six-inch guns.)

Old Chief Petty Officer Tom, our instructor for hydraulic systems, was a witty, enthusiastic, and friendly man. He would mix in jokes with his lecture to keep us awake. But it stopped working after a while.

One day, he said, "I really don't know how many girlfriends each of you have. I do not worry about your losing money or time over girls, but I do worry about your ship. If you feel sleepy, get up and walk around or go to the window and do some deep breathing."

Coincidentally, the rear window of the hydraulics classroom faced the Paymaster's office. After doing some deep breathing exercises at the window, one shipmate was very excited to report his discovery with us that evening.

"I was very tired and did my breathing exercise today with my arms occasionally stretched out fully. A Wren across the street thought I was waving at her. So she waved back. Do you know who the Wren was?" he said, showing off. "It was Pamela!"

(Translators' Note: Women in the Royal Navy were assigned to the Women's Royal Naval Service, abbreviated WRNS, but commonly known as Wrens.)

Only half-believing what he said, we set out to verify the truth on the next day. As soon as we entered the classroom, the lucky shipmate was eager to prove his story, so he started to wave his arms at the Wrens across the street. It was like ships busy exchanging light signals – transmitting and receiving, back and forth. By the end everybody was waving. Pamela also asked two or three other Wrens to help her to wave back. We all got very excited and did not notice that Tom had entered the room . . .

From that day onward, we would cure our drowsiness by walking to the rear window while facing Tom, but waving our hands from behind our back. We would also quickly glance over our shoulder when Tom was not looking. It was not important whether we received a reply, but it was the thrill of being able to do so. We all learned to be very skillful in sending our signals across the street. Whoever got an echo signal back from Pamela became the happiest and most boastful person for the day.

Tom, who had been in the Royal Navy his entire life and had seen quite a few ports, pretended he noticed nothing, but would occasionally wink at us with approval. Everyone was satisfied.

Through all this hand-waving, we got to know Pamela more. We finally became friends at the Base Club. We knew that after Hut No. 9 became famous, Pamela wanted to find out about us. But it was through our signaling exercise that we were able to know her in person.

Because of Pamela each of us was able to meet and get to know better a Wren of our own. Weekends at the Gunnery School took a romantic tune. However, Pamela was everyone's friend and so we all agreed that she would be off-limits to everyone.

Christmas was approaching as the seasons changed. The very first Christmas card we received was an interesting one. The envelope was addressed to:

Dear Sevens
From S.W.

Who could have sent us this card? We looked at the cartoon on the card, it showed Snow White having a Christmas dinner with the Seven Dwarfs!

The card came from Pamela, and we kept it our secret. In Western culture, a surprise gift is often valued.

During the winter recess, we were invited by families and friends to visit different parts of England. Upon our return, snow was on the ground and there was also a coal shortage that year. However, the furnace in Hut No. 9 kept us warm all winter.

Chinese New Year arrived and we asked Morgan for permission to celebrate the Lunar New Year. We proposed to cook Chinese food and invite friends from the school.

Boss Morgan agreed and thought this would be a good way to promote cultural exchange. He wanted to know who would be our guests?

"Of course, you are our number one guest," we replied. Morgan was very happy with our answer.

"In addition, here is a list of eight other guests." Morgan was surprised to see a list of eight Wrens with Pamela's name at the top of the list.

"You . . ." He glanced at us sideways and shook his head and then asked, "What shall we eat? Have you got bird's nest soup?"

It was a wonderful evening. First, seven men cooked a delicious meal. Second, since none of our foreign guests knew how to celebrate the Chinese New Year, they believed and did everything we told them. In appreciation for her Snow White friendship, we asked Pamela to be our female hostess.

After asking many questions about Chinese customs, Morgan raised this question: "What happens at midnight during Chinese New Year?"

We knew that in the West, midnight can be a wild event for dating couples. How should we explain this one?

Someone was quick to answer again. "At midnight, men sit in a tall chair and receive kowtow from young friends and female friends." All of us nodded while all our female guests all shook their heads in disbelief.

"Oh, that's a good custom that I will always remember," Morgan said jokingly. "Should we be doing it?" Laughter followed.

"Do you always fold your bed so neatly in China?" one Wren asked.

"Of course."

"Do all Chinese housewives do so?"

"Of course." Boasting is not a sin. All the girls shook their heads again.

"Don't worry, we will not ask you to marry us."

"If you do, we would not dare to accept." More laughter followed.

Just like our New Year's dinner, our training at Whale Island in 1947 ended as a success with fond memories. Spring came and snow melted. We were instructed to report to HMS Aurora to carry out her overhaul. We left Whale Island with many friends seeing us off. They also included our Wrens and Pamela.

Hut Number 9 and Pamela   33

   Time and memories come and go like wafting smoke in the wildness. Hut No. 9 and Pamela left us with fond memories. Is Hut No. 9 still there? Did Pamela ever get married? If the past can be revisited, I think all seven of us would like to go back to Whale Island and relive those special moments from our young life.

4

A Story of Seeing a Ghost

by Henry Yu-Heng Ho
from his book *Blue Water Memories,* 1964

A Horde of "Slothful Ghosts"

When considered within the entirety of Chinese naval history, the SS Chongqing, a cruiser that was previously the Royal Navy's HMS Aurora, was like a struck matchstick that burns brightly for a few seconds but is quickly extinguished. Many people, including many of my fellow comrades in the Navy, have never seen her. She has since faded out of our memories and is not even willingly recalled by most. Yet to me, this cruiser was special; she was the first ship on which I served. I had spent my blood and sweat to maintain and sail her. She in turn gave me my most glorious years. I cannot and I will not completely expunge these sentimental memories.

Half a year before the giving away of this "bride" from the British and while she was undergoing a major overhaul in the Portsmouth Naval Shipyard, I was among the first of the Chinese Navy to board her. As for any large warship that is undergoing a sizable refitting, the situation onboard was total pandemonium. With multiple gashes here and cuts there into her hull, you could while standing alongside her beam easily gaze into her heart – the engine room. Pipes and wires were either openly exposed or simply snapped apart, just like a cadaver in an anatomy laboratory. The British must have thought that we as workers of machinery maintenance and repair would be isolated and helpless once we left the U.K. So they felt they had to teach us as much as possible to support ourselves afterwards. Indeed, during this time we gained experience that we could not have otherwise in any normal scenario. We hoisted, inspected, and restored the whole gun turrets and the bridge. We tunneled our way into and worked within blind alleys and dead spaces that had not been occupied since this cruiser first left the shipyard where she was built. Hoping to bring home a perfect ship, we were hyperalert to every detail, fearing that even a simple screw not installed properly would become a burden after we returned to our country.

By all rights we were there to learn from the British engineers at the shipyard. But subconsciously, and slowly, we were becoming their supervisors at the same time, though we did not have direct authority to do so. Our managerial tools were limited as we could only threaten (by complaining) or cajole (by treating them to meals) to achieve our goals.

Our counterparts at the British shipyard were unmatched with respect to their technical expertise and know-how to visitors and guests from other countries. However, regarding their attitude to work, it is not an irresponsible insult to state that they worked like a horde of "slothful ghosts."

Many of these British workers were either older men who had served in the Royal Navy and had already earned their pension or locals who had worked at the shipyard for their entire lives. The British armed forces had recruited most if not all of their country's youth, leaving behind these "crusty fritters" of men to take care of needed work in the homeland. You should have seen how they spent their time in a typical day:

The working day starts at 8 o'clock. Without fail, no one is late. The clocking-in machine at the gate has no mercy at all. They board the cruiser in their customary uniform and gear, which never changes: a greasy yellow overall, an iron toolbox, and a daily newspaper under the armpit.

Onboard the cruiser, they find an empty spot – an alleyway, a vacant cabin, or somewhere with more space – and then sit down with a handful of friends. They lay hands on some hot water, fix a cup of milky tea, pull out sandwiches from their iron toolboxes for their breakfast. They then read the newspaper until 9 o'clock before reporting to their respective departments, looking already worn out from a hard day of work.

A Story of Seeing a Ghost

At 10 o'clock, British officers onboard are entitled to a break according to the timetable of the Royal Navy. During those supposed ten minutes, we too have taken up the habits of the Brits. We make a pot of tea, snack on a Swiss roll purchased from the cooperative, have a few smokes from the local 555 brand of cigarettes, and share conversation about our work. As for the civilian dockyard workers, they are employed by the Royal Navy so do what the Navy does. Thus, it was only right that they shared in this bit of a well-established tradition, even though it was not stated in their contracts with the shipyard.

This also became a tradition: any foreman or other important Brit who helped us with inspecting and repairing the ship's guns and other weaponry would be invited during the breaks to come to our cabins aboard the ship where we lived to "have a cuppa." We had several reasons for doing so. Firstly, it cost us almost nothing as the tea was paid for by the British government and we chipped in some money to buy snacks. Secondly, through these informal chats with the foremen we could pick their brains to learn more maintenance tips during the chitchat. Thirdly and most importantly, they had to follow our lead and get back to work when we yelled "Let's go" when the break was over.

By regulation, they should work from 8 o'clock to noon. But after the 11:20 a.m. broadcast, "Break time, clean the decks!" they will follow suit and mark the end of the morning, just like their fellow Navy personnel.

Fortunately, there is no other scheduled break besides "the seaman's afternoon tea" during the work hours from 1 to 5 o'clock. However, by "chopping the head and clipping the tail" of the afternoon shift, these fellows worked for only about half of the time. Every day when there were still forty minutes before they were supposed to knock off and go home, they would close their iron toolboxes, lazily stretch themselves, and say, "Tomorrow is another day!"

(Translators' Note: "Chopping the head and clipping the tail" is taken from a Chinese proverb.)

I had also heard that many had worked harder during the early years of this World War. Perhaps it is because with the war's end for Great Britain, they needed to soothe their high-strung nerves, hence their slothfulness. I can also recall a worker humorously saying, "Why should we be in a hurry? Isn't the war over already?"

An Ill-Fated Séance

Speaking of real ghosts, the U.K. is internationally renowned as a country of ghosts. Just like an old mansion, this country is home to endless tales of joy and sorrow experienced by historical figures who now cast haunted shadows after their passing. Its persistent dense morning fog and bleak climate must be conducive to the survival of phantoms, if they exist. Stories about apparitions appear unceasingly in newspapers. In popular magazines, you can frequently find many such stories published even with photographs. With so many examples and witnesses, it's rather difficult not to believe in them. Scientists with modern gadgets have even initiated expeditions to haunted houses in order to study these spirits. I daresay there are more believers in ghosts in the U.K. than there are skeptics.

Since a great number of ghosts live within the underworld in the British Isles and these ghosts are known to be very active, it is simply impossible for the living to ignore them. That being said, people here have nothing compared to the wizardry of Chinese exorcists such as Master Zhang [張天師] who have the power to dispel evil spirits. Besides, the ghosts in the U.K. are seemingly much friendlier. They don't have bulging eyes or stick their tongues out with a petrifying demeanor, nor do they have horrific or grotesque features like blood-oozing cyan faces with gigantic fangs. Their so-called haunting usually consists of a disturbing prank or a relentless attempt to seek attention. This also explains the common British fascination with supernatural encounters. There are regular "quasi-metaphysical" magazines that cover the topics of ghosts, research in spiritualism, and spiritualists themselves. In a nutshell, "ghost review," "ghost research," and "ghost hunt" have become their own schools of knowledge in Great Britain.

Although I do not follow or study ghosts, let alone believe in them, I have attended a séance following an earnest request. To relate this story of a live encounter with ghosts, I must commence with how I first made the acquaintance of a spiritualist.

Mason was a civilian repairman at the Portsmouth Naval Shipyard who was sent to overhaul the Flakvierling anti-aircraft guns on our cruiser. He was of a short build, with a stiff but honest-looking face. He was a man of few words, almost socially awkward. Since he was not one of the "slothful ghosts" at work, his solitude and formality made me empathize with him more. Although appearing initially surprised that I would reach out to him, he seemed to welcome my friendship. However, our

A Story of Seeing a Ghost

relationship was never as natural as what I had with the other British workers. There was always a sense of distance between us and an invisible barrier that is hard to describe. For instance, with regards to his manner of speech, he always addressed me as "Mr. Ho," and in return, I would politely call him "Mr. Mason." He always spoke in the so-called "Queen's English," never replacing "goodbye" with the colloquial "ta-ta." A sophisticated man such as Mason was not the typical boorish shipyard worker, but at the same time he lacked the straightforward candor of his peers.

Mason, if not an outright communist, must have been a leftist. He read the *Daily Worker,* which was nothing short of propaganda full of distorted facts and malicious attacks commonly adopted by the Communist Party. As such, this newspaper was confined to a much narrower readership than other papers. Unlike others at the shipyard, Mason never threw away the paper after he finished reading it. Instead, he handed it to us every day after finding out that we were unaware of its existence. People abroad buy and read the newspapers they wish to, and no one is forced into reading something they dislike. But who had the time to read that infuriating propaganda when we were living under the golden rule of "work hard, play hard"?

Mason once asked us a question at the dining table, "Tell me, would you guys take part in another war?"

I remember that a fellow sailor replied, "I would. In any war. If anyone is going to infringe on our national interest or sovereignty." The implication of this response was inclusive even for the Brits. After that, Mason rarely joined us at the dining table.

After recognizing that political proselytism would lead nowhere, Mason began to speak of ghosts to me. I was amazed by his extraordinary knowledge of ghosts as well as his perception of post-mortem spiritual existence and events of the afterlife. He once asked me, "Do you believe in the existence of spirits in this world?"

"Do you mean 'ghosts'?"

He smiled and said, "You may say that. 'Ghosts' and 'spirits' are merely different names that we are used to."

"Then I'll be honest with you. I don't."

"Well then, have you ever seen spirits?"

"I'd hope that I would have by now." This was intended as a civility to avoid a clearly negative response. Nevertheless, he seemed to perceive an unintended meaning in what I said.

"Very well. In the future, I must seek the opportunity to let you see one."

"I shall be glad."

I didn't take his words seriously, but the next day, he came back with a sincere invitation. "Mr. Ho, we have a gathering this Saturday that you must come to."

"Gathering? What kind of gathering, Mr. Mason?"

"It's what I had promised to you last time – a gathering of spiritualism. Would you consider whether you can make it? I have already spoken to the other members."

"Thank you, I think I can certainly come."

That Saturday morning, Mason reminded me once again as if it were the most important event ever, and we agreed to a time and venue to meet. Knowing that he was not the most popular friend of ours, I decided to keep his invitation a secret and not speak of my skepticism about it because I might be able to surprise my naval compatriots just in case I did encounter some ghosts.

I suited up and set off after afternoon tea. Mason lived in a residential area at the foot of South Downs, which is north of Portsmouth city. His daughter was married, his wife had passed away, and his house was partially rented out. No wonder he needed to seek ghosts to relieve his sorrows.

The gathering took place nearby in the home of an old lady named Becky, who was naturally the host of this small group. She wore on her small wrinkled face an enigmatic expression. The decorations and knickknacks that filled the house were old and gaudy – thick curtains, a shabby carpet, a Persian rug with long dangling silk pendants used as a tablecloth, a photo on the left, a painting on the right, a rocking chair, sofas of various lengths. As a stranger, I felt as if I could not breathe because the room was so cluttered.

I was somehow favored by Ms. Becky and she invited me to have a vegetarian meal. She said this diet promoted longevity. Around the same table, half of these people were vegetarians, and the other half at least approved of it. In a Western vegetarian diet, dairy, butter, and meat are prohibited, but chives, scallions, and garlic are not. Therefore, bread along with peanut butter, lettuce, potatoes, lentils, etc. were consumed. People say Chinese vegetarian cuisines are high-end and sophisticated delicacies. But this Western meatless meal that I ate literally tasted as if I were chewing wax. The host, Ms. Becky, seemed to be prestigious and powerful; she and her words were revered by the others at the table. She spoke at length about the arguments for parapsychology and provided several successful examples of conjuring spirits. It boils down to an old saying, "Faith makes things happen." It takes a pure mind to connect the living to beings from the underworld.

In the U.K., sunset in summer always occurs late in the day. When all members of this spiritualism gathering had arrived, a total of ten people, the event began. From the windows, we saw dusk falling, but it was still bright outside. To my surprise this conjuring was nothing like what I had seen from the movies. It wasn't as if everyone sat around a small square table unable to hold down its levitation with our hands when the ghost appeared. Neither was there a crystal ball revealing the entirety of the underworld or another dimension. Instead, everybody in the house sat in a circle. Ms. Becky, the witch, sat in a rocking chair, leading the séance.

The curtains were drawn, but the silhouette of each person was still slightly discernible thanks to the rays of light filtering through cracks in the curtains. Ms. Becky gave an especially detailed explanation of the conjuring method, perhaps because of me. At first everyone had to say a silent prayer and focus on recalling the dress, appearance, and mannerism of the dead whom you were trying to contact. When the spirit arrived, Ms. Becky would tell you and everyone else so that you could have a chat with him or her in silence or out loud. The most important thing, however, was to stay focused and keep your eyes shut.

The conjuring began. Everyone sat square with their hands on their knees and their eyes tightly closed. Ms. Becky babbled incantations in a trembling voice for a period of time. After a few moments she cried out to an elderly lady, "Mrs. Tuck, here comes the spirit whom you want to see. He's a gentleman, wearing a black top hat, with a walking stick in his hand. Can you see him?"

As we sat in silence, I was thinking of Mrs. Tuck, who'd sat opposite to me at dinner. Although her hair had turned silvery, she looked robust and healthy enough.

It was followed by the voice of Mrs. Tuck, "Yes, I can see him. He is walking toward me. Yes, he is Uncle Alfie. Ah! Uncle Alfie, I'm so glad to see you . . ." And the supposed conversation continued. I could tell from Mrs. Tuck's voice that she was completely immersed in this moment of imagination, talking with the spirit.

The activities of this gathering and their sequence were fully controlled and commanded by Ms. Becky. She was like a prison warden –

the wish of any visitor had to be delivered through her, and she would announce when time was up. Not everyone who attended the gathering could see their spirit. Perhaps it was because the underworld was occupied? Maybe Ms. Becky did not convey the message? Or the heart of the living was not sincere enough? I had no idea.

Anyway, Mrs. Tuck was a model example. She was followed by a few more of the many people who connected with the dead that day.

All of a sudden, Ms. Becky raised her voice and shrieked with apprehension, "There! A gentleman is coming – I don't know who he is." She paused. "I can't see his face, but – he is dressed in silken clothing. Oh! It is embroidered with flowers. He is not very tall. The style of his shoes is new to me. Oh! Mr. Ho, he's staring at you . . . and walking toward you. He must be the spirit you wish to see."

I was quite anxious because Ms. Becky's face and her look when she spoke permeated my mind's eye while my real ones were closed.

"Mr. Ho, can you see?"

"Where is it, Ms. Becky?"

"He appears through the windowpane as well, Mr. Ho. I dare say that he wants to talk to you."

Subconsciously, my still-closed eyes were led by her words to the windows. Though terrified to be caught, I very cautiously squinted a peek.

It was now darker in the house, and the figures of the people around me were hazy. Ms. Becky was still sitting opposite me; the tables and chairs were still there. I sized up each person. They were in the same position as when I first closed my eyes; the clock on the mantel was still ticking with a steady beat. Heck, what ghost or spirit was here?

I didn't realize how much time had passed. But the repeating words of Ms. Becky reminded me of the specter of the gentleman in silk.

"Mr. Ho, are you chatting with the gentleman?"

"Ms. Becky, I don't see anything."

Because of my throwaway remark, Ms. Becky paused for a moment as if she didn't know what to say.

"Oh! I see. This gentleman has obscured himself." Her words were simple, her tone was curt, just like this ghost of a Chinese gentleman taking an abrupt and rude departure.

After that, the final member of our group, Mason, had his turn. He met an old lady who was a neighbor who died almost thirty years ago. Being a well-experienced spiritualist, Mason naturally described this spirit as a lively being.

It finally came to an end after Ms. Becky closed with additional babble. Before we opened our eyes, we prayed again to send the spirits away. I intentionally waited until after the lights had been switched on to open my eyes and stand up.

Everyone regretted that I could not see the spirits this time. It could be said that this was somehow expected. Owing to the fact that I have zero knowledge of spiritualism, not to mention not knowing when to focus and purify my mind during the conjuring, it was easy for me to fail. But in the end, they all exclaimed that it was the first time that they had met a Chinese spirit, thanks to me.

Personally, I did have one regret. I wasted the prime hours of a Saturday evening on such an absurdity. What dullness!

I returned to the dock and my ship with more than a bit of resentment. Everyone, except for the sailors on duty, was out seeking and finding weekend fun. Without a word, I took my hammock and hung it up on its hooks.

"What's up? You came back so early!"

I didn't respond to that question.

"Where have you been? Did your lass stand you up?"

I remained silent.

"Oh! What happened to you? Seen a ghost?"

"I wish I did," I answered back, vexed. Then I jumped into my hammock.

5

War of the Roses

by Henry Yu-Heng Ho
from his book *Comedy on the Whitecaps*, 1965

"You know, if I did not love her, I would not have fought for her." As a result of this utterance, I was treated to several delicious dinners at the Russells'.

*****

He told me, "The first War of the Roses was fought in England in 1455 for nearly thirty years. It was a fight for the crown." He continued, "The second War of the Roses was also fought in England but in the fall of 1946 and it lasted only twenty-four hours. It was an international dispute, a contest involving both the Navy and the Army, a lover's quarrel, and a matter of national and personal pride . . ."

Bright lights illuminated our seaport. Ships were loading throughout the night as if they were working under daylight against a dark and devouring sea outside. To pass time before our supply convoy set sail for battle at Kinmen Islands [金門島] off the China coast, we leaned against the side rail of our naval escort frigate and chatted with each other. He took a last puff from his cigarette and skillfully flicked it over the ship's rail with his thumb and middle finger. Together, we watched the burning red butt tumble down in an arc before being swallowed by the dark water below. He continued with his story – a story you may regard as a trivial and silly incident during one's youth when every little thing seems to have greater importance than it really does.

*****

As an ally of the British, we traveled all the way to England to receive naval training toward the end of World War II in order to take over an ex-British warship. We accepted the risk of death in a foreign land during a time of war as a necessary possibility for experiencing an exciting journey. Although the British homeland had already tasted the bitter fruits of war, we found her people loved and appreciated all soldiers in view of the country's seemingly uncertain future. This warmth was also extended to Allied soldiers who came to help at a time of need. To make up for the loss of so many young British men fighting overseas, British women rose up and kept everything running at home. The few young men who remained were much in demand; it is hard to imagine their popularity with British women unless you have lived through the war. Even after the war a scarcity of men, akin to the chronic food shortages and omnipresent restoration of war-damaged buildings, became the norm.

Although England's reigning King George VI did not pay for our services, our benefits were the same as those of the Royal Navy Home Fleet. Best of all, we received the most satisfying leave privileges. They included routine weekends and longer ones because of holidays: Easter, summer leaves, Christmas, New Year's, sick leaves . . . During these leaves, transportation tickets and food ration coupons were fully provided so that we could have great fun. Those who were willing to sacrifice their leave and remain onboard received no credit, and one also had to work to eat. So we worked and played hard during our entire stay in England. It was a wonderful way to develop both our bodies and minds.

While we did much sightseeing in England and even in Europe during our first two years, we eventually settled down like the locals and lost our newfound curiosity for museum tours or "another sightseeing visit." Tall buildings and busy traffic no longer awed us. Instead, we rerouted our leaves to visit those small and scenic English towns with their tranquil surroundings and warm human touch.

On one occasion, my shipmate Liu and I left the Whale Island Gunnery School for a weekend leave, carrying our tan-colored British sailor's suitcase. Attracted by a worn-out tourism poster at the train station, we decided to visit Plymouth. This city was no more than three hours by train. Although she was well-known as a summer resort for the rich, we were sure that her hotels would offer discounts to off-season visitors. Plymouth was a seaside town known for her great beaches. Since she was not a seaport, we would not become bored by being around other sailors and their ships as we had enough of that during the workweek.

Upon our arrival, Plymouth appeared to be more beautiful than we had imagined. She was truly a serene and almost noble English town. There were many continental-style inns in the town, most of which were built along the hills and overlooking the sea. Looking through windows or just leaning against the porch, we could see the deep-blue seas gently stroking the sandy yellow beaches below us. The famous Plymouth Park occupied the town's entire southern hill. The park had carefully laid stone steps with small bridges crossing murmuring brooks, winding footpaths that led to reclusive spots, and colorful patches of flowers dotted among well-groomed grass lawns. Summer had passed, but Plymouth, with her charm and beauty, was resting quietly like a farm after an autumn harvest. We easily found a room in a luxury hotel at a frighteningly low price. Our floor was completely deserted except for our room. Other than a few elderly and lonely long-term guests, the rest of the hotel was also empty.

Liu and I finished our sightseeing the next day. Now it was nightfall with the beautiful city lights just lit. The night belongs to young people and their night lives among the colorful lights. After we finished a standard three-course dinner, neon lights guided us to a local dance hall. I should first explain how a dance hall in England differs from ours. There were no paid dancing companions nor table charges levied on top of admission fees. After a busy day men and women in couples or as singles could spend the evening dancing there as a means for easy and proper entertainment, much like going to a movie. The cost is comparable to the cinema. Beyond paid admission there were no extra charges or hustling waiters and waitresses asking you to spend more. Soft drinks and cigarettes could be easily purchased at concession stands. This was a true place for social dancing. Unless there were special circumstances, a simple "May I have this dance?" served as proper etiquette for the gentleman to invite a lady to dance. A man and woman could be fated to stay with each other after one dance or they would never see each other again after a single dance.

My friend and I followed our time-tested tactic whenever we visited a new dance hall. This was because most people, especially girls, doubted whether a foreigner, and especially one from the East, knew how to dance. If we were turned down for the first dance, then this apprehension would be reinforced and be in plain sight for others to see. Such rejection could then ruin the rest of the evening. Therefore, we would usually make an appearance next to the dance floor first. We may have smoked a cigarette and pretended that we were "old hands" or even chatted with a nearby chap to occupy time. We would then spot and target someone who was either not frequently asked or had a plain look. If this was correctly done and we were able to successfully demonstrate our dancing skills, the rest of the evening would be easy. No exception occurred that day.

My first invitation was extended to a girl who had stood by the floor for quite a while; she was also not bad looking. She looked almost Asian – a delicate oval face with cherry lips, a pair of bright eyes, smooth and fair skin. What impressed me most was that she did not have a hooked nose. She nonchalantly accepted my invitation but aggressively took the floor first.

After several steps, she spoke like a teacher who was encouraging a poor student, "You dance alright."

"Thank you, I've just learned." Experience had taught us to keep these situations light-hearted. In other words, don't be too serious in reply while always leaving room to entice more conversation. This was akin to patiently nurturing a piece of dough to rise with yeast.

"Yeah?" She turned her head around and looked somewhat in disbelief. I nodded and skillfully spun her several times.

"Where are you from?" she asked.

"China," I replied.

"Do people in China dance?"

"Our dances are much more difficult." I described to her a few dancing steps from Chinese Opera. It briefly attracted her curiosity before she quickly changed the subject.

"I saw you and your friend come in."

"Really?" I leaned forward and asked.

She opened her eyes wide and nodded. She also gave me a naïve, curious yet friendly smile.

"You know, this town is full of army, some air force, but rarely navy, especially foreign navy."

"You like the navy?" We moved toward a corner near the band.

She tilted her head and thought for a moment then playfully replied, "Your uniform is smart looking, right?"

This dance was nearing its end and we seemed to get along fine. It was time to make some down payment, so I continued, "Of course. If we were attending a costume ball, I would have worn an Admiral's uniform. Wouldn't you like that more?"

She laughed but did not answer.

"Could I ask you for another dance later?"

"I don't mind," she answered while still exhibiting her nonchalant attitude.

We finished the first dance and each returned to our corners. Liu noticed us and asked, "You two seemed to get along?"

"Oh, nothing serious except for some pleasantries exchanged. She is not bad looking," I replied. Liu nodded.

I asked her for the next dance. This time, we were more at ease with each other as we swapped personal information. Her name was Rose Russell and she was locally born. Rose had a mother and two brothers. Her family owned a fruit and produce store. She arrived that evening with her army date who did not like dancing or dance well. He had gone to the pub across the street for some beer.

After our second dance, I walked Rose back to her seat just as her date returned from the pub. Although his face was red from the beer, he seemed to be in a jovial mood. Rose introduced us and he led us to a larger table so we could get to know each other better. To even up my side, I signaled Liu to join us.

The music started again. Liu asked Rose for a dance while her friend Temple (his surname) and I spoke. Temple talked most of the time while I listened. He started by telling me that he was the boxing champion of his army company. He was busily preparing for the battalion competition. Temple bent his arm and asked me to feel his hard and strong bicep muscle.

"Do you box?" he asked after his long, cocky introduction of himself.

"Hmm, yes and no . . ."

"What do you mean?" I figured that Temple would be interested in anything related to boxing.

"Our fist-fighting method is not as limited as your boxing. We adopt many ways to strike an opponent. For example, there is Dian Xue, in which we use our fingers to attack various vital points of the human body. It can temporarily disable or permanently injure our opponents."

(Translators' Note: Dian Xue, also known as "Touch of Death," is a martial arts technique that utilizes acupressure to reputedly incapacitate or even to cause immediate or delayed death to an opponent.)

His eyes opened wider in disbelief and he asked, "Did you all learn it?"

"Yes, it is required for all of our soldiers and sailors. But we do not use it for competition."

"That's a pity." He did not get my meaning.

The dancing couple returned. Temple anxiously asked Liu, "Do you know Dian Xu?"

Liu looked puzzled. I quickly said to him in Chinese, "This guy is bragging about his boxing skills. I told him that we all know martial arts self-defense." Liu quickly caught on and gave confirmation.

However, the other party seemed still in doubt. Temple asked again, "Then show us how it's done?"

Our ruse was about to be broken, so I quickly said, "Not here. It is a skill that is very difficult to master. Like a physician you must first familiarize yourself with details of human anatomy."

Temple did not reply. Suddenly he yelled, "Ouch!" His body twitched as he almost tipped the whole table.

Liu opened both his hands and said, "See, this was just an example!"

It turned out that while Temple was not looking, Liu pinched the funny bone nerve on his elbow, which caused his arm to go numb and then be pained. Liu's smart move not only saved our evening but also convinced Temple of our ability. After this Temple generously bought us drinks and we had a great evening.

I thought that Temple and Rose were just ordinary friends, but he did get the last dance with Rose. I did get a chance to thank Rose separately and invite her to spend Sunday with me. I proposed a date that included lunch, visiting the parks, taking pictures and spending the evening dancing again.

But on the next day she failed to show up. Although Liu and I continued with our sightseeing, I felt somewhat disappointed and upset. At one stage I even contemplated returning to town earlier. After our supper I did not give up and suggested that we visit Trinity Church. This was because Rose told me the prior night that she usually attends the Sunday evening dance at this church. While the facilities there were sparse, tickets were cheaper and the dress code was casual. After having to endure the hardships of war, English people were thrifty.

Rose was there. She greeted us, "I knew you would come." She appeared pleased that I met her expectations. "My mischievous brother hurt his arm this morning so I took him to the hospital and missed our date."

Despite my doubts, I eagerly accepted her explanation – life should be merry with less second-guessing and worrying. I felt happy so long as I was with her that night. With Rose introducing us to everyone, we were already popular when the dance started. Although there were many army personnel, Temple was not among them. We had forgotten about him until he showed up halfway through the evening. He staggered into the church's side hall appearing half-drunk. This time he was followed by several army buddies.

He looked around and quickly found us. He walked over and questioned Rose in an accusing tone as to where she had been that day. Without waiting for her reply he also fired off a series of lecturing comments that both embarrassed and angered her.

He then turned around and with both hands on his waist asked rudely, "Sailor, are you in Plymouth looking for trouble?"

I wanted to help Rose explain about her brother's injury, but Temple gave me no chance to speak. His intimidating look also prevented me from offering any amiable response. Others were starting to notice us.

"We're here to spend the weekend. If you want to quarrel, how about we do it outside so we won't disturb others," I replied calmly with a stern face.

"Great." Temple turned around and told his buddies, "Like I've told you, these sailors are in town looking for trouble. Look, now he wants to go outside. Let's all go."

They led the way. Rose hesitated at first then hurriedly followed us. She pulled my sleeve and pleaded, "Please do not fight with him!"

I did not want to fight. I merely wanted to avoid arguing in public. However, my intention was obviously misunderstood! Even Liu gave me a stare, while Temple's buddies all appeared to feel great about my misfortune. Temple was by now drowning in arrogance.

Temple stopped beside a lamp post on the lawn. He pushed out his chest and said, "Now, I want you to tell me where you and Rose were today!" Such an inquisition prevented me from offering any meaningful reply because I would be viewed as being subdued by a bully.

"You have no right to ask!" I replied.

"But I have my right to make you talk." He moved into a fighting stance.

"What do you mean?"

"You know what I meant, come on!" He continued to provoke.

One of his army buddies, the self-appointed referee and peacemaker, offered, "Sailor, if you win, we leave and you keep Rose. If you lose, you leave Plymouth and will not trouble this town again."

Temple confidently agreed, "So be it." He held out both fists in front of his chest and leaned forward slightly in a fighting pose. He was ready to teach me a lesson.

Rose yelled repeatedly, "You two, don't fight!" I nodded in agreement.

Suddenly, Liu stepped between Temple and me and calmly spoke, "OK, we agree to settle this quarrel by force. However, we need to state our conditions. First, if Temple wishes to seek victory through boxing that we are not familiar with, we should be allowed to defend ourselves with Chinese martial arts. This means we can strike with our hands, feet, and use any other methods. Second, we should agree on a third-party witness. In this way, if someone sustains a permanent injury or even fatality through boxing or Chinese martial arts, there will be no seeking of legal compensation. Since my friend is very good with Dian Xue martial arts, an unpleasant ending is usually unavoidable."

His words cooled down the fighting air and chaos around us. They also seemed to suppress the other party's arrogance.

"What is a Dian Xue?" one army soldier asked.

"It is the way we use fingers to cause temporary or permanent injury." Liu now spoke like a drill instructor, pronouncing each word distinctly.

Rose seemed to have discovered how to stop this brawl. She quickly reminded everyone, "Temple should know. He was Dian Xue'd last night."

Temple kept quiet as he began to fear these mysterious Eastern secrets. His buddies were also less assertive.

"That was merely an example. Of course, it will be much more powerful in a real fight. Should we look for a third-party witness now?" Liu turned on the offense.

"It's not fair, I don't know their methods," Temple blurted, showing a sign of retreat.

"I think it is fair because we also do not know boxing."

More silence.

This time in a more polite and august tone Liu added, "My friends, we are in town for the weekend. We are in England to help you as allies and also find ways to win our own war. We are not here to make trouble. If you are willing to become friends, let us all go back to dancing. Otherwise . . ." Liu continued, "So, how about we let Miss Rose choose where we should go next – either we visit your party or return to the church ball for the rest of this evening?"

"Temple, I think you are behaving rudely tonight!" Rose hurled her displeasure at Temple.

Finally, we went back to the church dance less the army crowd.

*****

He paused.

"And then?" I asked

"There is a bit more to this story," he continued.

*****

It turns out that the Captain of the British warship that we were training to take over was himself from Plymouth. During the ship's hand-over period, we were often anchored off of Plymouth on weekends.

Once, while there, Rose brought her mother to meet me when I was ashore. Her French-born mother retained her charm and humor despite her age. During our first encounter, she pointed to the slope of Plymouth Park and complained, "Young man, she dragged me up and down these hills three times to look for you."

"I am sorry, Mrs. Russell."

"Oh, it's alright. I am very proud that you offered to fight for my daughter, I must thank you," she said with pride in her eyes. She looked at me and then at Rose. "You must love her very much."

French people were so romantic. God, there lay an extra bonus. I was happy to please her. So I said, "Mrs. Russell . . . after seeing you, I now understand how your daughter is so beautiful. You know, if I did not love her, I would not have fought for her."

As a result of this utterance, I was treated to several delicious dinners at the Russells'. Of course, I brought Liu with me.

*****

"And then?" I demanded.

"Hey, why do you continue asking about what happened afterwards?" Although my story-telling friend grew impatient, he did offer closure.

"Each ship has a home port. Although she is sailed around the world always carrying her home port's name on her hull, she eventually returns home like a leaf falling toward the root of its tree. I am the "ending" of this story. If you remembered what I told you about the shortage of men in England after the war, you would no doubt understand and not be surprised that Rose eventually married Temple."

6

Chang Feng for Ten Thousand Miles ["長風"萬里]

by Henry Yu-Heng Ho
from his book *Blue Water Memories*, 1964

Exactly ten years ago and far away on a retired British battle cruiser anchored in the Portsmouth Harbor of England, a Chinese publication named *Chang Feng* [長風 or Strong Wind] was born. It was published irregularly and printed on a mimeograph machine. Its staff, content, and layout were not much different than that of a small community or school journal. However, it was born of unusual circumstances and needs.

Firstly, the group of Chinese Navy officers and sailors dispatched to England to take command of several British warships had, by 1946, grown to be one thousand strong. Many of them, being thousands of miles away from home, were feeling homesick. A mere letter from home that had traveled over mountains and across seas was a precious item. Even a piece of scrap paper with a few Chinese words printed on it brought immeasurable comfort. Often, a piece of old newspaper was borrowed and hidden or fought over so many times that it became unrecognizable.

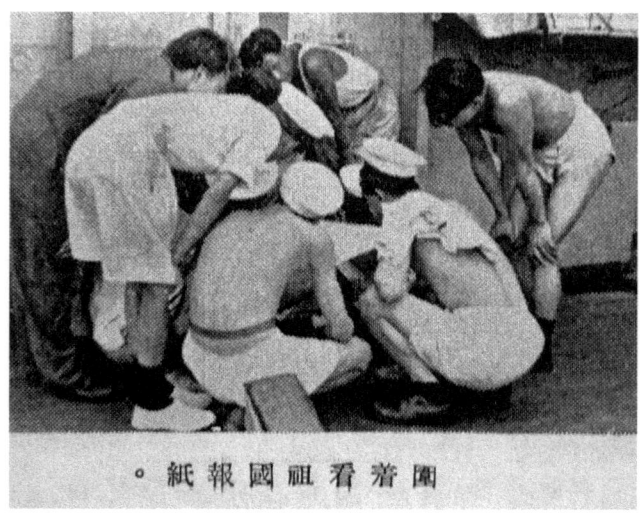

Photo: Chinese sailors gathered to read a newspaper from the homeland

Secondly, this group of one thousand shipmates came from all different parts of China and from many different professions. Many were complete strangers to each other. How this group got to know each other and bonded to become a cohesive team was a major challenge.

Thirdly, the group was only assembled after arrival in England and lived under the scrutiny of many pairs of blue eyes. Problems due to misunderstandings were bound to occur. Moreover, this group was then again divided and dispatched to different parts of England for various training while under urgent pressure to succeed.

Given these objectives and stressful requirements, a hunger for "spiritual food" naturally resonated into a need for a platform where learnings and ideas could be shared among the group. With the help and support of our training supervisor, Commander Zhao [趙志麟], a group of shipmates with editing and publishing experiences from college plus several enthusiastic doers emerged to meet this need. Commander Zhao even scraped up five pounds per week from the local British Naval cooperative store to fund the printing costs. Thus, *Chang Feng* was born on October 10, 1946.

(*Translators' Note: October 10 is the National Day of the Republic of China, which would eventually become Taiwan.*)

Chang Feng was published as three issues from the main training ship, the HMS Renown. By mid-November of 1947, many Chinese officers had completed their training and departed her. Most of them boarded what was later to become our ship, the SS Chongqing [ex-*HMS Aurora*] and commenced preparatory work for the eventual assuming of command of this warship. The *Chang Feng* group moved with them. Unfortunately, Commander Zhao was ordered back home to China, but he entrusted the leadership for this valuable publication, which he had helped to create to Lieutenant Commander Mu [牟秉釗]. Commander Zhao also fought for and received a twenty-pound monthly grant from our naval office in London to expand the activities of the *Chang Feng* group.

In December, we held a business meeting during which we finalized an organization charter, agreed on new proposals, added more staff, and divided the group into editorial and general affairs departments. The most important change was the addition of a semi-weekly *News Brief,* which focused on news from our homeland, major developments abroad, and military news.

The *News Brief* was widely distributed to the Chinese community in England and Europe to reach a wider readership. What was unique about our general affairs department, in addition to its printing and distribution responsibilities, was that its members also sponsored haircut and shoe-repair services. Later, we even added recreational activities such as a music band and ball teams. Thus, the *Chang Feng* group, which was originally organized for those of us who like to play with our pens, had morphed into a cultural and recreational organization.

By April of 1948, our navy's training office in England had closed and we lost our funding sponsor for the *Chang Feng* group. By now, activities for *Chang Feng* had moved on to the SS Chongqing. With overhaul work to ready the ship for transfer to the Chinese Navy accelerating, this left us with little extracurricular time. Besides, a light cruiser offered much less work space for the group than the battleship that served as our home for earlier training. As a result, *Chang Feng's* enterprising activities were also affected. *Chang Feng's* monthly journal was suspended after six issues. Instead, the group decided to focus on preparing a *Ship Transfer Commemorative Issue* [接艦專刊] to memorialize our days in England. Beyond this being a chronicle of the *Chang Feng* group, this *Commemorative Issue* included anecdotal stories. However, the *News Brief* continued right up to the time that we arrived at our home port in China.

Chang Feng frequently reminded me of how poor our propaganda efforts abroad were. Let us look at how things were in those days. On the

British Isles, the Chinese community was sizeable, but at the time there were only three other regularly published Chinese-language periodicals.

One was a typeset daily newspaper funded by the local Chinese community, whose name I cannot recall. Its first issue was launched with a grand and luxurious event that included fireworks and ribbon cutting. However, it quickly disappeared due to a lack of funds.

There was also the mimeographed *China Weekly* published from Liverpool. It included a variety of news and subjects and was printed as a full-sized newspaper. However, its contents were generally of poor quality and it lacked focus. It was expensive, thus suffered a poor circulation.

Finally, there was the mimeographed communist semi-weekly news bulletin also published from Liverpool. It was printed on a half-scale-sized newspaper and was free. It was routinely dispatched to readers based on a mailing list. It followed us like a walking shadow no matter which training ship or school we were at. Although we often trashed it or returned it to the sender, we were unable to shake off this shadow.

There was also an English-language weekly published by the Chinese Embassy. It was purely an official propaganda tool, available upon request. Its content was inadequate, and its consequence was limited.

Under these circumstances, our government lacked a clear and credible voice to influence the local Chinese communities. In a black-and-white propaganda competition, one should not always remain tolerant and silent. Most of us left China not so long ago, and we were more familiar with the situation in the homeland. While we understood or had experienced the perils of communism, how would the local Chinese people, who had resided abroad for a long time, be kept informed of what was going on inside of China?

The *Chang Feng* publications were widely welcomed by the Chinese community. Its content was more exciting, its news from China was more up to date. And it included inspirational news about top honors earned by our shipmates during their overseas trainings.

I recall reading a letter sent to my shipmate from a local Chinese reader. It roughly stated, "Thank you for the copy of *Chang Feng*. . . . While we were disappointed with news from home, we were able to learn good news through you. . . . Our homeland is like our parents. How can one not respect them? How can one always speak poorly about one's parents?"

(Translators' Note: Although World War II had ended, the Chinese Civil War between the Kuomintang-led government of the Republic of China

and the Communist Party of China was still ongoing and a source of news to Chinese people abroad.)

Once we boarded our ship, we were able to operate our communication equipment. Our radio comrade would perk up his ears whenever he heard news broadcast directly from China. Hence, when *Chang Feng* activities expanded, we immediately launched a semi-weekly *News Brief* to deliver in a timelier manner the latest news from home. As a result, our *News Brief* enjoyed a much higher distribution than the irregularly published *Chang Feng* journal.

With the help of the Navy, we were also able to dispatch our publications to Europe as far as the Mediterranean Coast. Thus, our *News Brief* became a dominant Chinese publication in Europe at the time. It offered a different voice to the overseas Chinese people. Over time, the communist news bulletins ceased being sent to Chinese Navy personnel. However, the *Chang Feng* group was not an overseas propaganda organization. Our publications eventually ceased when our tour of duty ended in England. Our consolation was that we had won support, praise, and belief from our Chinese friends abroad.

I will always remember a letter sent to me from a Chinese reader who lived in faraway Stockholm, Sweden. Although his Chinese was poor, his warm words truly touched my heart. "You will be returning to China and *Chang Feng* will be discontinued. Through *Chang Feng*, I felt the warmth of our motherland. Now I will return again to isolation and loneliness . . ."

I was not one of the founders of the *Chang Feng* group. I had been away for training and could only contribute to Issue No. 1 by mail. I formally joined *Chang Feng's* editorial department after the group moved to SS Chongqing. Each of the two departments had seven colleagues, and we all worked under Lt. Commander Mu, who also served as our Chief Editor.

After we finished our daily duties, we would crowd into the ship's laundry, which was the only free space available to our group. We, as self-appointed publishers or writers, would then work elbow-to-elbow to write, proofread, or compile the layout. Frankly speaking, we spent a lot of time working on the publication, but this space offered us freedom from the ship's rules. It was a place where we could chat freely or even play a trick or two on each other behind closed doors. Often, our lights remained lit after the ship's evening cabin inspections, so we felt rather privileged.

Within the *Chang Feng* circle, we became close friends. We had talented writers such as Xiao Yang [小羊], who wrote much like his personality – clear and precise but with depth and reflection. We had Hei Pi [黑皮], whose writing style was bold and profound. Then there was Chi Gong [癡公], who knew well and often incorporated classical literature in his works. He would sometimes teach us a bit of this skill.

Photo: Chang Feng editorial group. Henry Ho is standing, second from the left.

Wang [王耀埏], who was in charge of the *News Brief,* was the ship's radio operator. Every day, he would extract and edit relevant news from the ship's radio. Through his efforts, the *News Brief* always offered news ahead of anything else our crew had. He would also infuse stories of good deeds by our shipmates plus some overheard gossipy news to make the reading more interesting. *Chang Feng* publications took on Wang's personality – sharp, up-to-date, and lively.

The General Administration Department was led by Liu [劉正銑], who was born with organizational skills. He was both enthusiastic and active. He was also the driving force behind expanding *Chang Feng* from publishing to sponsoring cultural and recreational events. Lastly, let us not forget those shipmates who offered their free time to make copies by operating the mimeograph. All were hard-to-find and hard-to-forget buddies.

Since that time, we have been scattered in different places and have pursued different fortunes. Both *Chang Feng* chiefs are now promoted to Rear Admirals, while Wang and Liu have risen to ship's Captains. I continue to practice my insignificant writing skills as a hobby and have not thrown away my well-worn pen. However, I do believe that all of us who were involved, including our readers, will continue to remember *Chang Feng*.

But Ten Years Later . . .

Chang Feng did not meet with an unsung closure. The *Ship Transfer Commemorative Issue* has become our everlasting keepsake. We decided not to follow the approach of a common school yearbook or typical commemorative album. Instead, we asked our shipmates to write about their personal experiences during these memorable years. In my request for essays from our shipmates, I wrote, "We will print what you write. We will preserve what you are afraid to forget. While you may not feel these are worthwhile now, but ten years later . . ."

Photo: Cover of *Ship Transfer Commemorative Issue* for the warships SS Chongqing and SS Lin Fu

Now ten years later, as I read a borrowed copy of this book (mine was unfortunately lost), I discovered the weight of what I had unknowingly written in my invitation. I carefully regarded and examined each and every article and photo. Shipmates and stories from the past vividly came to life on the pages. You cannot hold back the passing of time, but spiritually (or in some other manner), this album is a testament to our "golden times."

As our ship sailed through the narrow Red Sea on our way back to China, the Gobi Desert of the Middle East on our left and the northern African desert on our right were like two ovens that boiled the sea like a kettle. During the day, a canvas top was erected and covered the ship's forward deck. A seawater hose below the tent cooled down our mates. However, work on *Chang Feng's* commemorative chronicle did not stop.

I will always remember Commander Mu's speech as he stood next to six-inch gun mount B: "Our shipmates have elected us to get this book done, so it is our duty. We will all carry a guilty conscience should the manuscript not be ready for printing when we arrive in Hong Kong."

So we worked with thick sweat-absorbing cotton towels placed under our bared arms. Large buckets of ice and salt tablets stood nearby. After days of hard work, we did not disappoint our shipmates and met our deadline.

This 168-page volume represents a potpourri of writings. These include the senior officers' addresses to the crew, lessons learned, technical papers, reports, travel notes, fictional stories, poetry in both modern and classical styles, you name it. Had we all worked harder, I am sure this book would have been even better.

An Italian female poet once wrote:
> *And dreaming through the twilight*
> *That doth not rise nor set,*
> *Haply, I may remember,*
> *And haply may forget.*

Accidentally, I remembered the past and fortuitously I forgot it again because we should not live in the past. However, through the eternal power of words, *Chang Feng* lives on in what Commander Mu wrote in the *Commemorative Issue:* "What will remain in our hearts are only memories and a reluctance to let go of the past! Only memories and reluctance!"

Chang Feng for Ten Thousand Miles 63

Photo: The first group of Chinese officers and seamen on the deck of the HMS Aurora in Portsmouth, UK, on May 6, 1946, prior to their being assigned to naval specialist schools throughout England. The full complement of crew for the SS Chongqing eventually numbered nearly 600.

Photo: SS Chongqing (formerly HMS Aurora) and SS Lin Fu (formerly HMS Mendip) anchored at Singapore, July 1948

China: 1949

7

Game of Checkers in Life
生命之棋局

by Peggy Ho using the pen name 珮琪
from Taiwan's *The Rambler* magazine (自由談), 1957

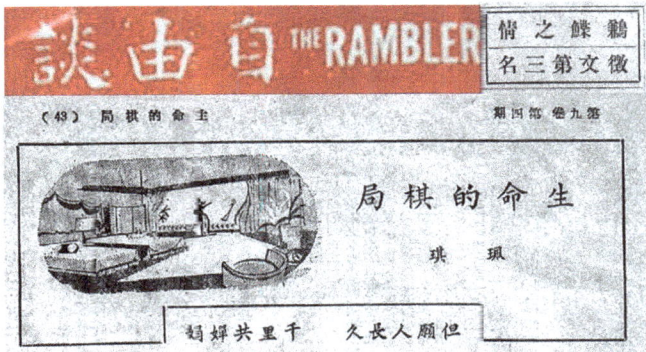

Awarded Third Prize by the 1957 Jian Die Sentiment Series competition (鶼鰈之情徵文)

(Translators' Note: Jian Die means "Inseparable Couple.")

*****

In terms of looks, he was rather average. He was a patient of mine when we first met. He had bloated cheeks after an operation for sinusitis. In terms of wealth, he owned nothing to his name except his navy uniform when I married him. In terms of social status, he was simply a junior naval officer. But that was before.

Yet, I married this man, and nine years have quickly passed. Since then, the world around us has changed greatly and our marriage, like a rich meal, has reflected all of life's different flavors – sweet, sour, bitter, spicy, and, of course with any navy man, salty. Although fate brought us together, we have since had a wonderful marriage. I made the right choice nine years ago. Now, I am studying abroad and thousands of miles away from him. Our past brings back many memories, but I have only one wish: "Though thousands of miles apart, may our love be forever as we share our dream under the same moonlight."

(Translators' Note: This passage is from a poem by the Sung Dynasty poet Su Dong-po 蘇東坡詩詞 *from* 水調歌頭 – 但願人長久，千里共嬋娟.*)*

In 1947, a pair of patients arrived at the hospital in Shanghai where I was working as a nurse. They were two navy shipmates returned from a winter battle in the Yellow Sea. They both served as crew members on a warship that was given to China by the British Navy a year ago. They both suffered sinusitis, which required operations at our hospital.

Honestly, I did not pay attention to either one of them as they were recuperating from successful operations. It was the day after the operations, a lazy Sunday afternoon, when I was on evening shift duty from 3 to 11 p.m.

"Miss, the patient next to me is bleeding," said this patient with the bloated face who appeared outside of my nursing station.

"Which bed?" I could not remember either this patient or his neighbor.

"Bed Number 9, we both had sinus operations." He had difficulties in speaking as his lips were swollen after the surgery.

I checked the medical charts. Their operations went well and there were no special orders from their attending physician. It was not unusual for some post-operative bleeding from the sinuses into the mouth to occur. Blood usually becomes mixed with saliva and in most cases nothing special can be done except to let it drain out. Besides, we were short of help on Sunday. This is not a life-threatening situation, but it can be scary to the patient. I could understand the anxiety from this fellow patient for his shipmate.

What impressed me about him was that he did not act like those easily excitable friends and relatives who had nothing better but to complain or give "expert suggestions" about others even though they knew not the first thing about medical affairs. He stood quietly and calmly next to Bed No. 9, ready to help me. But there was really nothing that he could do to help.

I then realized that he may also be bleeding or in discomfort from his walk to the nursing station. I told him to lie down and rest. He shook his head and squeezed a sentence through swollen lips

"But we are a pair and depend on each other."

The evening shift is generally light duty except for bed-checking rounds at dusk. After this incident, Bed No. 9 was careful to not leave his bed, and his recovery took a while longer. However, Bed No. 10 recovered quickly. He frequently visited my station to engage in conversation. I cannot say that I welcomed his visits, but neither did I dislike him.

One day, we ran out of conversation. He picked up a Chinese checkerboard sitting on the nursing station table and asked, "Miss, is this a checker game board?"

"Yes, do you know how to play?" I had just learned the game and was enthusiastic to try my skills.

He looked at me and with a smile said, "Never played it before."

"Then I shall teach you."

I opened the checkerboard and explained to him the rules. Indeed, he did not know how to play the game. Although I was also a new player and hardly ever won games, he was worse than me. He could only foresee two moves ahead each time. Often, he thought his move would have disadvantaged me, but in fact it actually created more bridges for me. I would try not to show my anxiety over some easy winning move that he had but did not make. He just could not see these winning moves. Often, I won, leaving him with one lonely piece left behind.

I should not look down on a beginner, but he was quite bad in Chinese checkers and often displayed a silly smile to cover his embarrassment. In any event, I was happy to play with someone whom I could easily beat.

My acquaintance with Bed No. 9 was improved as he recovered. One day, while I was pondering a move in a game of checkers with Bed No. 10, No. 9 came in. After watching our games for a while, he said, "Be careful, Miss, he is a well-known checkers player on our ship."

No. 10 quickly nudged his indiscrete friend and blurted out, "Don't talk nonsense. I just learned the game from Miss . . ."

His shipmate then grasped the situation and quickly grew silent. I saw the whole situation for what it was. In my heart, I was annoyed and a bit angry with him and thought that he should not have cheated me.

However, there are different perspectives on everything. After work, I lay in my bed and thought about this troubling incident. After all, checkers was only a game. Why should I think so much over this matter? Did he let me win just to please me? Did he deliberately make those bad moves to help me to win? All those silly moves he made . . . But by doing so, he showed himself to be a very considerate person with a gentle personality and a clever head. This was one of the reasons why I married him.

So, who won the checkers game? Our married life somewhat reflects this checkers game. We do not argue over different opinions. He always lets me know that he respects and will abide by my ideas. However, I will then usually compromise due to my being in a good mood after "winning."

During the second year of our marriage, we saw our neighbor's children playing Chinese checkers. He enthusiastically asked me, "How about we borrow their checkerboard to play? I remember you always beat me."

"I won? You must be joking! You not only beat me last time but also won my heart. No more playing with you."

He then put on his silly smile again. We never did play Chinese checkers again.

Of course, we did not get married simply as a result of checkers. After his hospital stay, he returned home to Hunan province, which he had left when he joined the Nationalist Chinese Navy. Civil war was around us and things were changing quickly. The Communists had taken over northern China and were threatening the Yangtze River in the South upon his return to Shanghai. While the city was under constant rumors of siege, we were immersed in romance.

We celebrated Christmas in 1947 at the Kai Fu Hotel [凱福 飯店] on North Sichuan Road with dinner followed by the hotel's famous costume party. We drank dry gin that he brought from his ex-British warship. As we left the dance hall he was wearing an Egyptian fez, one arm holding the bottle while the other arm locked with me. We sang Christmas songs amongst the late-night street crowd as he escorted me to my midnight shift at the hospital. I began to wonder whether I was delirious from this sailor's salt in my blood.

When spring came, his ship was called for sea duty again. On a foggy early morning, I walked him to the river, waved good-bye from the navy pier, and saw him off in a boat that headed for his warship anchored at the mouth of the Huangpu River. I was both sad and worried. Navy life is often unpredictable. Who knew when we would see each other again?

But God kept him for me. His warship, SS Chongqing, defected to the Communists in the north before dawn. He returned to the city with a heavy heart. With the ship went everything he had. He was despondent and depressed for quite a while. I, on the other hand, was very happy inside as he had not inadvertently fallen into harm's way. He was still with me.

Although his ship was forever lost to him, it did not defeat him as he found an assignment on another ship. However, he loved that first ship and his navy. He would cry like a child when he thought about the ship's mutiny. He loved to travel, and since he lost everything but the uniform he wore, he was anxious to reconstruct his world again even during this difficult time of civil war.

To me, his ship took away his belongings, but not his kind spirit and clever mind. He never made any empty promises or boasted of himself, which many men would do to win a girl's heart. I found safety in his sincerity during this troublesome civil war. Things could have been worse, but no matter what they would become better.

In 1949, panic flared up in Shanghai as the Communists approached the city. He was quickly reassigned on a warship heading for Taiwan. I saw him off again at the riverside pier, but with less anxiety this time because Taiwan was to be the revival base for the Nationalist government. At this time, I had decided that I would marry him and I would no longer leave him in times of need. For this reason, I left Shanghai and proceeded to Taiwan ahead of my own parents.

I do not know what constitutes a perfect marriage. I only know that our marriage has given both of us a peaceful and beautiful life together. I cannot recall any faults or rifts; I remember only building a family together and sharing with each other both good and bad moments. We do not have a life of luxury. We waste not and do not go hungry. He encouraged me to further my studies and helped me to gain admission to study nursing in the United States. In a way, we were hard at work in tilling our own farm. While we do not wish for a pot of gold in our field, we do find a plentiful harvest there for us each time.

As a navy wife, I, along with my peers, have different daily experiences than other wives. We are more sensitive to changes in the weather; it causes us to wonder whether our loved ones are safe at sea. When strong winds blow through tree branches, we worry about its impact on our ships in the ocean. When rain strikes our windows at night, it strikes at the heart of every navy wife. Are our loved ones sailing against the wind and rain out there?

In this war across the Taiwan Strait, where is his ship? What is he doing? When will he return safely? There are no answers. After a while, we become used to hiding our worries and learn to push our thoughts inside. We pretend that their patrol missions are routine tasks. We suppress our overjoyed feelings when they return home safely.

In 1954, when everyone was busy preparing for the New Year, he was called to Taipei for a special assignment. It was the time of the Dachen Island invasion by the Communists, and a dark cloud hung over everyone's mind. I understood why and where he was sent. The besieged Dachen had attracted worldwide attention.

(Translators' Note: The Battle of Dachen Islands [大陳群島之戰] *was a struggle between the Nationalists and the Communists for the control of several archipelagos just off the coast of Zhejiang, China, during the Chinese Civil War in the post-World War II era. It was part of the First Taiwan Strait Crisis.)*

Photo: Henry Ho (left) on Dachen Island, 1954

There was no news from him for one month. This was unusual. To lessen my worries, he usually called to let me know he was safe as soon as the ship arrived back to homeport. No matter where his ship was, he would also find a way to get a message to me every two to three days.

I was very worried when the Nationalists began to evacuate Dachen Island. There were very few details in the news.

I celebrated the "joyous" Chinese New Year by praying and hoping. I had to put on a smiling face to our friends who visited our home during the New Year to wish us well. But my nights were long and worrisome. I felt bitter at being treated unfairly.

Finally, he returned home safely. His face looked tired, and he was disheartened. His hair was uncut and his beard unshaven. His uniform was dirty, and there was mud on his boots. His ragged appearance spoke for the hardships he experienced at the front. At that moment, my complaints were trivial compared to the hardships he had gone through.

"How are you at home? Was our boy good?"

"Fine," I answered with a light smile, "and you?"

"Fine," he answered with a light smile.

Such a simple greeting masked and extinguished months of loneliness for him. That light smile also represented our understanding, sympathy, consoling, and everlasting love for each other. Years at sea can force upon a mariner a tough and reserved character. They can also shape a navy wife to show extreme patience and endurance.

Marriage is a contract under the law without a guarantee of reward to each spouse. It is also a covenant without mutual conditions or compensation. Although I sacrificed all for him, at the same time, I enjoyed all he had to offer.

On a Chinese marriage certificate the following fortuitous words are written:

Today, radiant peach blossoms bloom.
A heavenly time for marrying and to start a family.
May there be many children for you two to prosper with in years to come . . .
[看今日桃花灼灼.
宜室宜家
他年瓜瓞綿綿, 爾昌爾熾 . . .]

Western marriage vows describe the married couple's obligations:
... from this day forward, for better, for worse,
for richer, for poorer,
in sickness and in health,
until death do us part ...

At the time of this writing, the U.S. Midwest is covered in gleaming white winter snow. Outside, it is very peaceful and clear. Looking back to my first eight years of marriage, it has been a warm, happy, and satisfying time. Although money, looks, and social status were not my criteria for marriage, my experience has proven that these are indeed not important. The real meaning and purpose of life are much more.

Photo: Wedding of Henry and Peggy Ho, Taiwan, 1950

God has been generous and merciful to me. I continue to pray for His blessing and care for my family. At the same time, I also pray, "May all lovers be brought together into marriage."

願天下有情人終成眷屬.

Photo: Henry and Peggy Ho, Taiwan, 1964

8

A Life of a Postman

by Henry Yu-Heng Ho
from *Postal Services Today,* 1989

Publisher's Preface:

Yu-Heng (Henry) Ho is a writer well known in Taiwan and abroad. He is also the eldest son-in-law of Deputy Director-General of Postal Services Mr. Ping-Wen Hsueh [薛聘文] (1901-1989), who recently passed away. On July 14, 1989, the Taipei Postal Museum dedicated a room to exhibit Mr. Hsueh's personal collection of books, artifacts, and manuscripts, which were donated to the museum. The dedication ceremony was presided over by Director General Wong. Mr. Ho returned from the United States to attend the ceremony and contributed this article as a family remembrance of Mr. Hsueh. Through this article penned by a great writer, we are able to understand more about a man who dedicated his whole life to our Postal Services through both his work and family life. Our magazine is honored to obtain the publishing rights to this article, and we will also keep it as a valuable first-hand archive in the museum.

*****

Mr. Ping-Wen Hsueh was my father-in-law. He passed away at the age of eighty-eight on the fifth of March 1989 in Taipei. To commemorate Sir's life-long contributions to the development of China's Postal Service, a special exhibit has been commissioned at the Taiwan Postal Museum to display his works and artifacts. His lifetime of work will now become a part of China's postal history. As his son-in-law, and on behalf of his surviving family, we wish to thank the Postal Bureau's current and former officials for honoring Sir today. I would also like to share Sir's family life as well as his words as a supplement to the Exhibit. With such an honor bestowed upon Sir by the Bureau, I am sure that his spirit in heaven would be pleased.
(Translators' Note: "Sir" is a salutation used by the writer to emphasize respect.)

Photo: Our grandparents, Mr. & Mrs. Ping-Wen Hsueh, in Taiwan

First Acquaintance

When I returned to China in 1948 from England, I was posted in Shanghai as a young naval officer. While in Shanghai, I met and fell in love with Sir's eldest daughter, Peggy. Although the civil war between the Nationalists and the Communists had broken out, Peggy and I were deeply in love despite war clouds and an abundance of anxiety around us. Upon learning that I had decided to sail upstream on the Yangtze River to Hunan province to visit my frail grandmother, Peggy hurriedly arranged a first-time meeting between us and her parents. Her intention was obvious. And so one evening I dressed up and headed to Sir's home for dinner in Shanghai's Jing-An District.

According to Peggy, her father worked for the Postal Bureau. He was especially busy as the Nationalist government was preparing to evacuate to the southern provinces after having lost several key battles to the Communists in the north. I felt uneasy about this dinner. I had heard that Shanghai people tend to reject those who are not their own. Besides, I could neither speak nor comprehend their local dialect. Therefore, I felt that I already lost half of the game before making my first move. Besides, there were countless tragic stories about romances torn apart by the war. If Sir deferred in giving us his blessings, I would lose the remaining half of the game.

Peggy's home was tastefully decorated and clean. My first impression of Sir was that of a stern but kind man. He politely asked about my past three years of naval training in the United Kingdom and about my family. He spoke to me in a relaxed and friendly manner, which helped to ease this apparent son-in-law interview. While I could not understand everything that he said because of his heavy Shanghainese accent, we pretended to understand each other and carried on.

During our chat, my future mother-in-law was busy directing the household helpers with dinner preparations. I felt that her eyes were always looking at me whether she was nearby or at the far end of the room. It made me uneasy, but she never interrupted my conversation with Sir. Besides, I would only understand less than 10 percent of what she said because of her heavy native Chongming Island accent. As the evening wore on, I was able to converse with her through Peggy or with help from Peggy's younger sister.

My mother-in-law was clearly in charge at the dinner table. From time to time, she instructed me to taste every dish served. It was a multiple course meal with chicken, duck, seafood, and pork. I knew these ingredients were not easily obtained during the civil war. She repeatedly asked me to eat a thick soy sauce-covered dish known as "ng" [厄] in her native dialect. I had no idea what it was, but so long as I ate something whenever she spoke to me, we got along fine.

After we left Peggy's home, I asked her how I did. Peggy told me that her father did not like to display his true emotions. He frequently praised everyone and rarely showed displeasure openly. This was the mark of a fine gentleman, a trait that cannot be taught or easily assumed.

To satisfy my curiosity, I asked Peggy what was the "ng" dish? My question stunned her for a brief moment before she laughed and said, "Oh, 'ng' means fish. I told Mother that you love fish." For the next forty years, I was always treated to a "ng" dish when we visited our in-laws.

Reacquaintance

Upon my return from Changsha, the capital of Hunan province, where I was born, the cities near Shanghai had fallen to the advancing Communist troops and Shanghai itself was in danger of being besieged. My father-in-law had flown to Guangzhou to personally attend to the evacuation of the Postal Bureau to southern China. I again asked Peggy about my scorecard from our earlier dinner.

"Consider yourself lucky to have received a passing grade . . ."

Several days later, I left Shanghai with the fleet and sailed to Taiwan. Peggy arrived later by herself with a few pieces of jewelry given to her by her mother as the Chinese yuan [paper currency] had devaluated to little or no value.

I later learned that at the time, my father-in-law was entrusted with a large amount of government funds to finance the evacuation of the Postal Bureau. During the war, "borrowing" a bit from funds such as these to secure safe travel for one's family would have been an understandable act. Such a thought of placing family before his official duties never occurred to Sir. The Postal Bureau was his career and his life. He was also a man of strong integrity.

The next time I saw my father-in-law was in Taipei after the Nationalist government had moved to Taiwan. Peggy and I traveled from the southern naval base at Tso-Ying to northern Taiwan to ask for Sir's blessing of our marriage. He gave us his blessing in his usual composed manner. He was unable to attend our wedding due to a business trip to Hong Kong. Understandably, rebuilding the Postal Service in Taiwan was an urgent matter that benefited us all. Besides, Peggy's mother and several of her siblings were still trapped in Shanghai. For the time being, they were being cared for by his colleagues.

Sir treated us to a dinner at a well-known Western restaurant in Taipei. Afterward, we went to a bookstore as he offered to buy us books as gifts.

(Translators' Note: Those of us who grew up with our grandfather can testify that we stood a far higher chance of receiving books from him rather than toys.)

I tried to imagine how Sir felt with his wife and children trapped behind the enemy line while he carried on with his job. We can only guess the struggle within him behind his calm exterior.

Our wedding was hosted by Peggy's uncle and aunt on behalf of her parents. After paying off banquet costs with all the gift money and most of our paltry savings, we could not afford a real honeymoon at the popular Sun Moon Lake Resort [日月潭]. Instead, we celebrated our honeymoon in a one-room naval dormitory.

Dedicated to Changes

After our wedding, the civil war gradually came to an end and we accepted Taiwan as our "temporary" home. Life returned to normal. All of us were grateful for being able to avoid the cruelty of war, and each of us individually began to plan and build our future.

Sir and his family eventually settled in Taipei. With the help of other postal workers, my mother-in-law escaped from Shanghai to Taipei with only their eighth daughter and ninth son. Number three son and number five daughter continued their studies at Tsinghua University in Beijing and at Fudan University in Shanghai, respectively. The eldest son, who worked for the China Merchant Shipping Company, also moved to Taipei.

The Postal Bureau in Taiwan evolved with its move and led the government agencies in management reforms. At the request of Mr. Y.T. Chang [張亞卿], branch head of the Zuoying [左營] City Postal Branch, I taught English to local staff after work. This job made me a local celebrity, and my mailing address was simply: Henry Ho, Zuoying City, Taiwan, Republic of China. Peggy and I needed neither a street address nor a postal code to receive our mail because local post office staff knew us all too well.

During this period, I learned more about the Postal Bureau system and witnessed their professionalism and disciplined approach to work. Such a culture enabled them to become a top-rated public service in Taiwan.

Continuous improvement of the Postal Service was always on my father-in-law's mind. Any person, thing, and matter related to his business attracted his attention. Many changes were conceived and planned by him from his office or his study at home. During leisurely strolls with his grandchildren, he was known to inspect the green mail-collection boxes for peeling paint or to ensure their markings were correctly displayed. The business of the Postal Bureau was very much a part of Sir, and anything related to it became an extension of him.

Teaching the Youth

Peggy and I moved from Zuoying to Taipei in the early 1960s. This allowed us to visit her parents more frequently. Through these visits, I learned more about how Sir managed his work and family life.

A man who had chosen what is good and did not compromise [擇善固執], he lived a healthy life governed by self-discipline as his daily activities ran like a clock. He was an early riser and played tennis for many years. Tennis was his primary, if not only, sport and hobby. This hobby also contributed to his good health in later years. Even when he retired from tennis because of age, he would still take a bus to visit the tennis club early in the morning. At the club, he would walk around and chat with old friends or simply watch the young players with great joy.

After lunch, everyone at home knew to be quiet during his nap time. After dinner, everyone knew it was his time to watch the evening news on television. After the news, he would retire to the study to attend to his homework on postal business.

For his diet, my mother-in-law's home-cooked meals focused around his preferences. Salty Chongming [崇明] dishes such as deep-fried peanuts with their skin cooked to just the right color was a daily necessity. Sir did not smoke, nor did he drink alcohol, preferring instead to take plain water with his meals. Occasionally during a social occasion, he would break this habit and show that he could easily hold his own in drinking with close friends and relatives. This reflected his competitive and face-saving character. However, he would never outdrink others as it was not his nature to show off.

At home, my mother-in-law's life revolved around him. Although they had household help, she personally attended to all matters at home that involved him. She occasionally liked to sneak away for a game of mahjong. If caught, she would behave like a guilty student who had been caught reading a novel in the classroom. She would insist on leaving or finishing a game so that she would always be home to greet him when he returned from work. I have never seen him angry or openly displeased with her over mahjong games, nor any other household matters.

Nevertheless, everyone at home always did their best to please him. If there was one exception, it was his granddaughter. Whenever she cried or pouted, he would drop everything and hurriedly come out of his study to pamper her. This proved to be a humorous scene as we watched a typically composed senior awkwardly try to console his very young granddaughter, Xiao Ling. Through his willingness to risk self-embarrassment in these instances, we think he was actually demonstrating one of his sayings, "Always be full of praise and you can change a piece of rock to gold." [句句都說好, 石頭變成寶.] This was the parenting standard that he expected of us.

Photo: A family gathering in Taipei (circa 1964) at the home of our grandparents (seated) with Henry and Peggy Ho (center standing) flanked by two sets of aunts and uncles. Five of an eventual total of fourteen grandchildren are shown, including David and Peter Ho (center on the floor).

Later in life, when his grandchildren were studying abroad or whenever he would hear good news about their achievements, Sir would personally select a trophy from a jewelry shop in Taipei and send it by air post to both acknowledge and encourage them. He never gave a gift of cash or frivolous trinkets as a reward.

When Peggy and I bought our first home in the United States, Sir personally copied the entire 516 words from the *Family Teachings of Zhu Zi* [朱子家訓] in perfect calligraphy. He then had it framed and shipped thousands of miles as a housewarming gift to us. Mounted in our living room and next to the Zhu Zi teachings was also a pair of frames for a well-known couplet, which was also personally written by Sir. It reads, "百年燕翼惟修德. 萬里鵬程在讀書." This couplet may be interpreted as "Generations of good deeds protect the family like a giant eagle's wing shielding its young. Life's journey of ten thousand miles is a quest for knowledge to glorify the family." His encouragement and expectations were reminders that our journey in the New World was like walking on ice such that we had to step carefully. When my two sons graduated from high school and college, I directed each of them to take a photo next to this framed couplet so we would never forget his teaching of our heritage. *(Translators' Note: In the days of old, this fourteen-character couplet was customarily hung at the family shrine within one's home to remind the younger generations to always remember to do good deeds and to study hard to get ahead.)*

Photo: David Ho at his college graduation in 1974 standing next to one of two parts of the calligraphy couplet brush written and framed by our grandfather

Filial Piety Remembrance

Although I have never met Sir's parents, we learned about them, especially his mother Madam Zhou, through informal conversations. He would vividly describe the love and care provided by Madam Zhou, such as how she took care of him during many late hours of study during hot summer and cold winter nights. This was the only time we saw tears in his eyes, as he expressed regret for not being able to better care for her. He inherited Madam Zhou's parenting methods, which were based on encouragement rather than strict discipline and emphasized love rather than spoiling the child. Through these stories we could see how his characteristic persistence that came across in his academic and career pursuits emanated from the teachings of Madam Zhou.

To honor and remember his parents, Sir would gather his children and grandchildren to observe the anniversary date of the death of his parents. On these days, fresh flowers, wine, and cooked food were offered together with bowing and silent prayers within his home's garden. This was always a solemn ceremony conducted with great reverence to demonstrate the sincerity of ancestral remembrance.

As his "half son," and over the forty years I knew him, I think there were two things that I did that pleased him. One was that I saved all my stipends during a naval tour in the United States to finance Peggy's furthering of her nursing studies in the U.S. To show his support for and to commend our effort, he took our elder son, David, into their home while Peggy was abroad. This was a great help to us as young parents as this lessened Peggy's anxiety and allowed me to carry out my naval duties at sea without worry. The other matter was that after much searching, I obtained copies of rare postal history records for him at the Library of Congress in Washington, D.C.

The first matter echoed his lifelong view that the quest for greater knowledge and skills is always more important than material wealth or pleasure. Hence, it was absolutely appropriate to travel ten thousand miles to gain knowledge. With his support, Peggy was able to complete her three years of nursing studies in Cincinnati and we later were able to return to the U.S. and develop the life that we have today in the States. The second matter also made him happy as all matters related to the Postal Service were important to him. These rare postal records helped him to bridge a gap in his writings about China's modern postal history. Like a successful treasure hunter, he genuinely cherished these documents and often reminded me about them.

Homeward Bound

When my mother-in-law passed away in Taiwan in 1978, all of his children in the U.S. were worried about his living alone. We proposed that he move to the States so we could take care of him. In the spring of 1981, he visited each child's home on both the East and West coasts. During a walk at dusk with him at my mushroom farm in Pennsylvania, he explained that although he was happy that all of his children welcomed him, he felt that Taipei was his real home. Although his personal collection of postal memorabilia could be shipped to the States, he would still miss many records kept in the Postal Bureau's archive in Taipei. He felt that his health was still good enough to live independently. Besides, the flights between Taiwan and the States were convenient. So he asked us not to worry about him.

I did not attempt any further persuasion, nor did I try to change his mind. I knew it would be very hard to do anything once his mind was made up. Besides, his reasoning was rational and had been carefully thought through. To him, life is not just about maintaining comfort. Life is not about staying still, but rather about continuously shaping one's environment guided by one's expectations for life. To him, continued work, i.e., writing, was the best way to demonstrate his vitality.

Sir also said, "I am very satisfied with my life as my children are doing well and even my grandchildren are doing well." After he returned to Taipei, this same saying often appeared at the end of his letters to us. He did not want us to worry about him. Every time I read these words, I was motivated to prove to him that we, like the rock in his adage, could indeed be transformed into a golden treasure.

After this trip, however, Sir never returned to the East Coast of the U.S. As Peggy and I sent him off at the airport, we sadly watched him walk alone into the departure gate and turn around to wave his farewell. He was over eighty. Although he walked with healthy strides, we could see those fading years on his back. Tears flooded Peggy's eyes for a long time while guilt gripped our hearts as his children.

I tried to console Peggy by referring to my conversation with him in Pennsylvania.

"I think Dad made the right choice. Staying at his children's home too long would compromise the dignity and freedom he had as the head of household for all these years. Despite the bonds from flesh and blood, an occasional indignant comment from a daughter- or son-in-law or a grandchild's mischievous behavior could result in wounds that may not be easily mended.

"You should take comfort that he and we are very fortunate. Besides us, Dad also has a large and warm family in the Postal Bureau. In that family, he is well respected and cared for by many in the same manner as we would care for him. In that extended family he is like a fish swimming freely and happily.

"At his age, long-distance travel would be a burden for him, and it would be a sin for us to make him do so. However, when he steps off the airplane in Taipei, he is returning to a perfect home. There, he will sit in his study and be absorbed in the work that he loves. He will be surrounded by friends who share his interests. He will be happy. His children in the States may not offer such happiness in his late years."

Before we finish this tribute, the family wishes to thank Madam Huang-Lin Cha Mo [黃林查某], who meticulously took care of Sir during his later years. Madam Huang-Lin is from a well-to-do family and has successful children of her own. But having a great, generous heart, she chose not to resign from a challenging job when she otherwise could have. The death of Sir causes her great grief, and we are truly touched by her tears of sadness. Madam Huang-Lin's care and help are truly blessings from the Almighty.

My wife Peggy was able to be with Sir during his last moments. She witnessed him passing away peacefully, a reflection of his great satisfaction and joy over a lifelong career with the Postal Bureau. We sincerely wish that Sir, as one who led a life of a postman, will be long remembered through the dedication of this room at the Postal Museum.

Taiwan: 1950 to 1964

9

A Gunnery Petty Officer and His Trumpet

by Henry Yu-Heng Ho
from his book *Blue Water Memories*, 1964

Our ship's Captain was a Commander by rank. This was his third command of a warship. While we may not have liked him, we were all thankful to have him as our leader, especially during times of crisis. He made us feel safe and lucky.

The ship's officers felt that the Captain's order to dress up for meals was excessive, especially when sailing in the hot and humid subtropical Taiwan Strait. The enlisted men also disliked the Captain's rule requiring all hands to stop their work and salute whenever he passed by.

A new order arrived from our Fleet Command: all brass fixtures on deck must be painted over to prevent enemy airplanes from spotting their reflective glare. We were all more than willing to carry out this order as it eliminated the traditional and tedious task of polishing brass. However, our Captain added an additional command: Gunnery Petty Officer Du would no longer be allowed to play his trumpet on deck.

You may wonder why Du did not play his trumpet below deck. There were two very good reasons. First, at least a dozen sailors were usually resting or sleeping in their quarters after a night of exhausting duties. The sound of a trumpet would not have been welcoming music to them. Instead, they might have been expected to bash in anyone's head if they were disturbed. Also, although everyone except for the Captain loved Du's music, the crowded crew's quarters were simply not big enough to accommodate Du's concerts.

Du's trumpet had its own legacy. He purchased it in America when we were dispatched to receive this surplus World War II warship from the U.S. Navy. We also learned that during his high school days, Du was nicknamed "Harry James" in the school band. While most of us felt that Du could have had a more promising career in the Navy, he loved only three things in life: sleeping, fixing naval guns, and playing the trumpet. Someone once suggested to Du that he take the officer's qualification examination, but he replied, "If everyone wants to be an officer, who will be enlisted?"

We all knew the real reason why the Captain restricted Du from playing his trumpet on deck was not because of the hazard of its glare revealing us to the enemy. A tough guy like our Captain simply does not like cushy stuff such as music. Fleet Command's new order provided our Captain with the perfect excuse to stop Du from spiritually threatening the Captain's desire to lead a tough ship.

Du was obviously distressed by this harsh new order. He went straight to the Captain.

"Captain, sir, permission to play my trumpet at a place where enemy airplanes cannot spot it?"

The Captain gave him a stern stare while seeing several seamen cast curious glances at him from afar. "OK, beneath this spot," he said while pointing to a spot on the lifeboat deck that was shaded by the bridge wing. He then turned around immediately and retired to his cabin without looking back.

Du was well known on this ship not only for his musical lips but also as an acknowledged expert in his trade, which was naval weaponry. With only one or two looks at any weapon, Du would figure out quickly what made it tick. He was a very tense person during the ship's firing exercises, regardless of whether we fired live or dummy rounds. Du's station was anywhere and everywhere whenever the guns went off. When our three-inch main gun developed a problem, Du was already fixing it before the ship's fire control officer knew about it. You would see him busily removing unfired or jammed shells, quickly taking pieces apart, and putting them back together. After a repair, he quickly disappeared to look elsewhere for trouble.

Over several years, we conducted many patrols in the Taiwan Strait as well as in all four seas off the China coast. We fought the Communists at the mouth of the Pearl River, off Hainan and Zhou Shan Islands. We carried out embargo assignments against mainland China, protected our mine-laying vessels, and bombarded shore targets. There were too many missions to recall, but it was hard to forget Du's soothing music wafting through the gentle breeze on a moonlit night or his spirited trumpet brightly calling the dark-green sea under a clear blue sky.

During his afternoon off-duty hours, Du would often bring his well-polished trumpet and stick his head into the radio room. With a usual wink at his radio specialist buddy, he would place a popular music record on the phonograph. Music would then be piped through the ship's broadcasting system and Du would settle leisurely at his "assigned spot" on the life-boat deck. With his eyes closed and back leaned against the bulkhead, his trumpet reverberated through the salty mist and into our hearts.

The rest of us would automatically gather around, light a cigarette, and listen with our eyes closed. Some of the younger seamen, while still dressed in their greasy work clothes, would start to dance. Seeing them dance, Du would add a few trembling notes for excitement. Sometimes he played his favorite songs, while other times he played tunes that we chose. These were the happiest times aboard our ship. It was also the time you could hear the Captain's door shut with a bang. Du answered it with a wink, to which we replied with an understanding smile.

Music aroused our memories, our fantasies, and our hope. Not just to sailors, but also to any common man, music can bring back memories of places we have visited, people we have met, and stories we have heard. Music can also take you away from reality. As we closed our eyes, Du's music brought us away from this warship and onto a sea-cruising yacht full of bathing beauties on its sundeck, each with a seductive smile. When Du played a dark tone, its heavy-hearted notes reminded us of a weeping girl who lost her lover or of the sorrowful sighs of a widow. Sadness and sympathy would appear on the faces of those who heard him play.

Du's music even made the officers more human. Once, I caught the Captain hiding behind the stern gun wall listening to Du. However, he quickly disappeared. I feel sorry that our Captain was not able to enjoy the beauty of the music like us. Du's trumpet made us forget those rough days at sea.

Another patrol. It was dusk. A deep orange-red sunset painted the western horizon toward China like an oil painting of hell. Du was playing the "Last Post," with its solemn notes and heavy-hearted touch. Suddenly, the sound of General Quarters awoke us all. Gunnery Petty Officer Du, being most sensitive to the sound of the battle alarm, immediately stopped playing and ran toward the ship's forward main gun with his trumpet.

Our anti-aircraft gun, already at quarters, opened fire over the orange-colored water to the west. Two enemy planes flew in low and, with the sunset behind them, started their attack. Within one minute, all of our ship's guns were firing. The intruders suddenly pulled up and strafed us with their machine guns. A bomb fell within five meters of the stern and splashed up a tall column of water. A cacophony of gunfire quickly filled the quiet sea surface like the random firecrackers heard during the Chinese New Year's Eve. Battle on an otherwise calm and innocent sea raged on.

From the bridge, I saw Gunny Du rush to the stern anti-aircraft gun like a raging bull. With one swift pull, he removed the overheated gun barrel and threw it into the cooling tube. A new barrel was quickly installed, and the anti-aircraft gun continued to fire.

One enemy plane was shot down and blown into smithereens in the fiery sky. However, the ship's bow was also hit by a bomb; our three-inch forward main gun was destroyed. All of its crew were either dead or severely injured. Fortunately, damage control quickly secured all the water-tight doors, and our ship survived the hit. As the second intruder retreated, he was hit by our three-inch stern gun. His plane flew away with a long trail of black smoke behind its tail and later crashed into the sea. Its pilot was left to report to the Dragon King of the Eastern China Sea.

After the battle, the Captain ordered damage control to commence and our medics to attend to the wounded. Out of caution, a state of General Quarters remained until after sundown while all lights onboard were blackened throughout the night. No one had the stomach to eat or the heart to talk. Although we shot down both intruders, we paid the heavy price of comrades irrevocably lost.

Fleet Command gave us permission to return to base for repairs. While cleaning up the forecastle deck the next morning, Du's trumpet was found among the spent shell cartridges. There were heavy-hearted debates as to whether we should bury it at sea with Du or keep it in memory of him. The Captain came by as if he wanted to say something. When he saw the trumpet, he looked at everyone and left without saying a word . . .

At noon, a sea burial was held with honor guards with the crew in formation at the aft deck. Traditionally, the "Last Post" bugle call was to be played. No one except for Du could express our anger and sorrow through these notes, but he now lay under a brand-new flag. After the rifles fired their salutes, we raised all five stretchers so that five valiant warriors who gave their lives to their motherland during troubled times could be returned to the sea that they loved. Five splashes appeared momentarily next to the ship's hull, and the sea then returned to its silence embracing those who are now finally resting in peace.

Soft weeping was heard among the burial detail and from the crew. An injured deck seaman, in his extreme grief, wanted to join his comrades but was restrained by others. He was known to be a tough guy among us, but now he cried like a little child. This incident caused many to also shed their tears.

Another sunset. Boatman Petty Officer Han mounted Du's trumpet on a finely made wooden frame. He brought it to the boat deck where we normally gathered to hear Du play. All hats were off as we watched Han mount the trumpet above the spot where Gunnery Petty Officer Du used to sit and play his trumpet.

The Captain came down and saw us standing out of formation on the boat deck. As he turned toward Han, he saw the trumpet being mounted.

"Take it off!" he said. No one moved, no one made a sound. The only noise heard was the waves rhythmically beating against the ship's hull. Several seamen held their fists tightly and stared sternly at the Captain.

"Take it off, Mr. Han! Put it there," the Captain ordered while pointing to a conspicuous spot in the middle of the ship's upper signal deck. He then turned around and headed toward the bridge without looking back.

I walked to the ship's stern and sat on her depth-charge rack. I lit a cigarette and watched her wake drag behind us. I was not aware of when the night sky crept in. I turned around and glanced at the bridge, knowing that the Captain was at his usual chair staring out over our ship's rising and falling bow. I knew that Gunnery Petty Officer Du's trumpet had become this warship's proud symbol. I could not help but feel very empty and melancholy.

10

Holy Water

by Henry Yu-Heng Ho
from his book *Comedy on the Whitecaps*, 1965

Translators' Note: This is an account of an actual wartime incident that Henry Ho was assigned by fleet headquarters to document. PC-104 was a PC-461 class submarine chaser originally built in Nashville, TN and commissioned by the United States Navy in 1943 as PC-1247. It was transferred to the Republic of China in 1948 in Subic Bay, Philippines and renamed PC-104. This ship was manned by a crew of sixty-five officers and enlisted sailors. The characters and events described in this story are real.

*****

"Rise and shine! Rise and shine! Fresh water available! Fresh water available!"

Daybreak – patrol craft PC-104's duty petty officer walked through the hatch door of the enlisted men's quarters. He sounded one long, shrill whistle from his boatswain's pipe before repeating his verbal orders. He then pounded his fist several times against the aluminum skin of the personal lockers before considering his routine supervisory duty completed.

"Damn you, stop shouting and haunting us like a ghost!" mumbled gun spotter and Seaman First Class Lin [林錫欽] with his usual pet phrase. Lin then turned around to face the ship's steel hull and continued back to sleep.

Indeed, the little frigate PC-104 had been on patrol in the Taiwan Strait for nearly three months. After having valiantly won three engagements, compliance with ship's routine orders understandably had become lax as the ship continued to sail.

"Fresh water available" is a powerful enticement for a sailor to get out of his bunk. During these harsh patrol tours, life's greatest pleasure could be simply derived from the two ladlesful of rationed fresh water . . . used first for gargling, then for face washing, shaving, mopping down body sweat, feet washing, and, finally, for rubbing the odor out of smelly socks. Eventually, but with a feeling of guilt for "wasting" a valuable resource, this half-bowl of now-dark slurry is helplessly dumped overboard.

"Anyway, only people can dirty the water, no water can dirty people." Such was one of Lin's many logical arguments.

Lin was like a celebrity on PC-104. He was smart and quick-witted, but stubborn. He was talkative – tough and unreserved. He was a good writer and also served as a reporter for the Navy's newspaper. As a journalist he had connections with news media outside. How could anyone, in this fewer than one-hundred-person small society of ours, treat him differently? When Lin was mischievous, we forgave him. When he put on a carefree, innocent, and humorous face, he was the most popular person on PC-104.

Our ship was now heading back to base with the crew busily spreading this good news like sparrows chirping on a tree. After we docked, regardless of where or for how long, there would be shore leave! We could at least visit a snooker hall. We could at least visit the Navy store to eat ice cream and flirt with the pretty shopkeepers. We could at least take a bath. We could at least wash our dirty underwear. We could at least . . . there were just too many choices for "we could at least" for us.

Lin finally got up from his bunk before breakfast. He was in a cheerful mood. He thought about his own "I could at least" plans. He "could at least" report to everyone the news about the ship's return to homeport. Lin ebulliently picked up his face-washing bowl and walked to the crew's shower, which was by now empty. He pressed the spring-loaded shower faucet, but not a single drop of water came out. What a disappointment. "This guy's timing is more accurate than the tide!"

"This guy," in Lin's mind, was petty officer Tang from the engineering team. Tang was also assigned to implement oil and water rationing during combat. Tang was a tough and meticulous person with only duty, order, and regulation running through his head. Tang kept a tight grip over the ship's oil and water rationing. Tang was all business; he was uncompromising on top of having the mule-like temper typical of folks from Hunan. Those who wanted to scoop more than their share of fresh water stood a better chance of threading a camel through the eye of a needle. Whether inside or outside of China's waters, the Navy always selected this type of person to do rationing duty. Otherwise, why would the U.S. Navy have nicknamed this job the "Oil and Water King?"

(Translators' Note: Hunan is a province in central China.)

By now food steamers in the ship's galley were emitting fragrant aromas from freshly steamed breakfast buns. Like a fish drawn to bait, Lin next headed toward the galley. Although he was not hungry, the aroma made Lin contemplate something else. He stuck his head into the galley, which had only one seaman who was busily tending to rice porridge. They greeted each other with knowing smiles. Lin raised and waved his washing bowl with his right hand. He then made an inquisitive but peculiar gesture while pointing to the empty bowl with his left hand.

His counterpart, who now had the only access to fresh water on this ship, smiled and nodded. Lin accepted his helping hand and with a winning grin offered, "I won't forget this. I will thank you once I get paid for my next article."

"My brother, let's talk about it when you get paid." The galley seaman uttered the truth.

Unfortunately, the road taken by enemies is narrow as they will surely meet. Before Lin could carry away his fresh water, Tang entered the galley carrying with him his Oil and Water King's trademark – a box wrench for opening and shutting faucets.

With his eyes fixed on the bowl of fresh water in Lin's hands, Tang asked in a harsh voice, "What are you doing?"

"I was just getting some water to wash my face." Lin managed to squeeze out an apologetic smile through his thick lips.

"Wash your face? Water distribution stopped thirty minutes ago! The ship's Executive Officer has issued strict orders against getting water from the galley . . ." Tang always treated such challenges to his authority seriously.

"My brother, don't be nervous. Aren't we heading back to base? There will be plenty of replenishment soon," Lin replied in a relaxed tone.

"Return to base? Fresh water replenishment? Can you guarantee any of that? How many times have we had to sail out right after we entered port? How many times have we had to untie mooring lines right after we just docked? We are at war. Who can guarantee what happens next?" Tang's Hunan accent became heavier and heavier at the end of each sentence.

"OK, no need to say more." Lin never liked to be lectured. He shifted from defense to offense and proposed, "As soon as the ship is docked, I will get two pails of fresh water from shore and return it to you. If our ship will not dock tomorrow, I will not consume any water tomorrow, OK?"

"Return to me? It is not my water. It belongs to the ship. Let's all understand this. I did not lay down the rule. This is the ship's regulation!"

Lin put down his bowl on the kitchen counter. Exasperated and with his hands on his hips he pleaded, "Then please tell me what you want?"

"Pour it back into the water tank!"

"What if I don't?"

"Then report yourself to the Exec."

"You can report me to the Exec, I am too busy." Lin picked up his water bowl and started to leave.

"This won't do!" The pair of round eyes on Tang's already large round face grew wider while both crevices formed between his nose and each side of his cheeks deepened. Tang did not want the other party to simply march off. He grabbed Lin's arm, which caused half of the fresh water to spill.

Lin threw down his water bowl and followed with a fist punch. This blow was both the crest and the terminus of their dispute. The rest became a matter for a court-martial.

The Executive Officer convened the court-martial in accordance with navy regulations. This was a simple case and of course there were many witnesses. Against regulations Lin privately took fresh water. He also struck another sailor.

After a discussion with the ship's counselor, it was agreed that Lin should be sentenced to confinement for five days. Prompt action to stop any violence in a close-quartered environment is a must. The Exec, in fact, had written the figure "5" on his notepad before the trial.

"Did Tang state this incident correctly?" the Exec asked Lin.

"Yes." Lin's answer was simple.

"Did you privately take fresh water?"

"Yes."

"Did you strike him and he did not strike back?"

"Yes."

"Do you accept a disciplinary action?" Both the Exec and the counselor felt this kid exhibited the diehard spirit of a soldier.

"Yes, I do."

The Exec looked Lin over and then nodded. Lin had a tall and thin frame yet was full of childish stubbornness. The Exec displayed a barely noticeable smile of satisfaction. He then handed Lin a punishment of five days of confinement. Lin accepted it willingly.

"Lin, do you know that you are at fault?"

Lin did not reply. He merely looked away toward the temporary surgical-light mounting bracket hanging in the middle of the officer's wardroom.

"Then you don't feel you were in the wrong?"

"Report to Exec! I did not say that."

"You also did not say you were at fault." The Exec was well aware of this big kid's temperament. "Why don't you carefully think it over? The sentence will be carried out after we reach base."

Lin saluted the Exec. As Lin was about to leave the wardroom, the Exec spoke again, "Lin, do you think you owe Tang an apology?"

"Report to Exec! Sir! I already received the discipline I deserved." Lin saluted again and exited the wardroom.

Just as Tang had predicted, PC-104 docked at her base only long enough to pick up some officials who were in a hurry to get to the frontline islands. She turned around and followed the western sunset out.

As part of the southern patrol squadron, PC-104 had won three engagements since the beginning of the year. Morale grew stronger with each victory. Only in frontline waters can heroic naval actions be shown. This time she was again dispatched to the active Liao Luo Bay.

(Translators' Note: Liao Luo Bay is located off the southern beach of Kinmen Island, the site of several naval engagements fought in the late 1940s and 1950s.)

The stomachs full of resentment left over from Lin and Tang's morning mishap temporarily gave way. Like their shipmates and officers, they were focused on the same singular thought, "Great, it is time to get into the action again."

The sun had set and the fleet's lead ship radioed the squadron leader's nightly orders. There was nothing unusual and all were to remain on battle station standby as we did every night. The lights-out order was given. Every hatch, door, and window port was tightly shut for another all-night battle station alert. Inside the ship's compartments, hot and humid air mixed with everyone's anxiety. Those who were not on duty could be found chatting on the open deck. Everyone was waiting for the night curtain to cover the sea, the fleet, and everything around us.

Darkness did come. The crew's chatter centered on today's headline: "The Oil and Water King versus the Crownless King."

The Oil and Water King felt irritated as he stood next to the stern depth-charge rack letting it hide him. "Help each other in the same boat" is a common motto and practice for all shipmates. Quarreling and upsetting others is never a good thing. Besides that, after the morning incident, Tang quite regretted his stubborn temper.

Deep down, Tang actually liked this young conscript and shipmate from Yi Lan County. Lin had a lively and enthusiastic personality. Although Lin was impulsive, he was a straightforward lad. Tang recalled a hard-to-forget and embarrassing, at least to himself, incident when the ship last docked at Kaohsiung. In an article he wrote for the Navy news, Lin effusively praised Tang for having rescued a drowning child. Lin's dispatch earned Tang a merit medal. Tang asked himself with a degree of self-blame and shame, "Is this how I repay his good deeds?"

(Translators' Note: Yi Lan County is a rural section of northeast Taiwan. Kaohsiung is a port city in southern Taiwan.)

Suddenly, Lin appeared, looking like he had found his favorite object. "Brother Tang, here you are. I have been looking all over the ship for you!"

Against the dark night, Tang could not see Lin's apologetic face. However, he could sense it from Lin's voice. Tang was at a loss for words.

"About today, please accept my apologies." Lin gently patted Tang's shoulder and then left his hand there. Tang's remorse, mixed with this unexpected apology from Lin, overwhelmed him. Tang felt even worse than when he was punched that morning.

"You know the kind of person I am, but I'm getting better after joining the Navy." Lin stared down at the foamy stern wake shimmering with a speckled bluish glow that trailed behind the ship. He continued, "Anyway, I was wrong today. Let's forget about my silly idea to pay you

Holy Water

back for the water spilled. But don't forget, I will make it up to you after I receive my writing fees."

As he became more touched, Tang continued to be lost for words. Though darkness covered each of their faces, Tang dared not turn his head around to look at his shipmate.

"Well, I must report back to my spotter's station on the bridge. I made up a toilet break excuse to find you; Chief Zhu is temporarily on watch for me." Lin again patted Tang's shoulder and said, "Don't mind me too much. You see, to demonstrate my sincere apology, I have not washed my face since this morning. See you later."

Tang remained silent. Suddenly, he thought about one thing and blurted, "Xiao Lin." He firmly grabbed Lin's arms as if he were afraid that Lin would slip away and exclaimed, "Everyone said that you stood overly exposed during battle stations. It is not good to ignore your own safety. Will you be more careful?"

(Translators' Note: "Xiao" literally means "little" and in this case conveys that Lin is Tang's younger brother.)

"Of course, I will," Lin replied in a thankful tone. "But don't forget that I am a spotter whose job is to be the first to identify friend from foe. Besides, it is a joy to see an enemy being destroyed! I am also a news reporter. If I don't stand higher to be able to see farther, how can I write? I really must go now or Chief Zhu will call me lazy again."

Lin's dark silhouette disappeared behind the forty-millimeter Bofors anti-aircraft gun. Tang stood lost in his thoughts for a while before hurriedly walking to the officer's wardroom.

"Report to Exec!" He did not wait to receive permission to enter. Instead, he moved apart the curtain and barged in.

"Yes?" The lanky Exec turned his head away from a pile of paperwork.

"Lin just apologized to me."

"I am not surprised." The Exec smiled slightly.

"I think it was I at fault today."

"No, you weren't."

"But I wronged him."

"No, you did not."

"He asked for my forgiveness."

"What did you say?"

Tang thought about it, but he hadn't said much to Lin. "I told him to be careful during battle."

The Exec gave a knowing smile as a sweet and harmonious feeling of family swelled within his heart.

"Exec, permission to request . . ."

"Speak freely."

"I would like the Exec to waive Lin's five days of confinement. If not, let me serve his sentence instead."

"Oh, I am afraid that I cannot rescind a court-martial. Only the Captain has such authority." The Exec regarded Tang's disappointed face and continued, "However, I will forward your request to the Captain. Lin is a good lad, but the young man needs to learn that bullheaded behavior is not tolerated no matter where he is."

Fleet command sounded the battle station alarm for the ships in Liao Luo Bay [料羅灣].

All hands now manned their stations. Layers of watertight doors were tightly shut. All guns were fully loaded and ready for action. The crew above deck anxiously searched for targets while the crew below deck apprehensively waited for the guns to roar. Anxiety was most unbearable during this game of waiting.

Targets were sighted – not just a few, but many. Gunfire erupted. It wasn't just loud; it screamed continuously.

We need not describe more how PC-104 heroically fought and won this famous battle. Everyone on her lived through a wild nightmare as enemies approached insanely from all directions. The fighters' eyes became bloodshot red. Gun barrels turned red from overheating. The entire deck was red from blood.

Over half of the crew were injured or dead. The ship's hull and superstructure were riddled with holes from bullets and shells. Flooding to the lower compartments caused severe listing such that the ship's starboard deck was now even with the waterline. Propulsion was lost, resulting in PC-104 having to be towed back to port by a friendly [another ship from the fleet]. But they won. None of the eleven enemy torpedo boats and gunboats lived to return.

Holy Water

Photo: PC-104 under tow after suffering battle damage and casualties in Liao Luo Bay

Lin died a brave warrior. He died fulfilling his duties as a gun spotter and as the ship's reporter. He died with honor – worthy of his life and without regrets.

Tang survived. He moved from compartment to compartment and continued to carry out damage control repairs. He isolated damaged oil lines, he fought fires and flooding, he moved the injured below deck. His body was smeared with oil and seawater. His shoes were lost and his clothes were torn without his knowing when and how it occurred. Thick oil and grease covered his arms and face while seawater bleached any exposed skin.

Those who were alive and those who were able to move worked hard toward one common goal while crying out, "Don't abandon the ship! Don't let PC-104 go down!"

Their ship was rescued. Friendlies arrived and allied forces also came to help. The ship's crew was now able to take a breather to tend to matters that had been postponed.

The dead were moved from their posts – either as intact bodies or as much as possible. They were neatly laid on deck; each one was covered with a white sheet and the flag. Those who had earlier received first aid were further tended to in order to lessen their pain or give more comfort. Those who survived started to think about themselves.

Tang stood transfixed next to the forty-millimeter gun mount. He looked like a zombie because exhaustion from no sleep, no food, and no drink over the past twenty-four hours had gotten to him. He was pondering a question that he would never understand, "Lin is dead?"

The Exec declined an offer of food from the U.S. Navy but instead asked for fresh water.

This water tasted better than that from any fresh natural spring and was more precious than the sweetest dew. It was ice water to boot. Who would have thought that a cup of water could be such an elixir? A cup of water offered such luxurious enjoyment . . .

"Tang, would you like some water?" yelled the officer who was liaising with the U.S. Navy's Lieutenant Davis as Davis came aboard to assist with damage control.

"Water?" Tang awoke from his daze, "Oh yes, water! Water!" Tang quickly walked over and filled a paper cup with water. He did not drink from his cup. He piously held the cup with both hands as he carefully walked along the listing deck. He uncovered the flag and white sheet then knelt next to Lin.

"You see, to express my apologies, I have yet to wash my face." Tang repeated this sentence like a tape recorder, over and over again, to Lin. He poured some water onto Lin's pale-white face. He then pulled a corner of the white sheet and gently cleaned Lin's lip while repeating quietly over and over, "Please forgive me . . . please forgive me . . ." Lin's face was as cold as was the ice water. Lin's body and Tang's heart grew colder and colder.

The cup was eventually emptied, but droplets of water continued to fall gently onto Lin's face. Not realizing this, Tang continued to look at Lin and wipe the peaceful face before him, not realizing that the droplets were his tears.

Nearby, Lieutenant Davis observed this act and was puzzled. He asked the Exec, "What is he doing? Is that a cup of holy water?"

"You . . ." The Exec began to explain but stopped as tears welled in his eyes and flowed down into his throat. He quickly turned and faced away, "You will not understand, my friend."

Photo: Details of battle damage to PC-104 after being towed back to port in Taiwan. Standing in front of the bridge is its surviving Captain, who was Henry Ho's fellow officer.

11

Translator's Foreword to the Chinese Version of *The Story of The New York Times, 1851-1951* by Meyer Berger

by Henry Yu-Heng Ho
February 1965 (1st ed.) and September 1972 (2nd ed.)

When the Chinese version of *The Story of The New York Times, 1851-1951* was ready for publication, I was truly relieved. I looked forward with joy and contentment for this colossal volume of more than 600,000 words to finally be available to the Chinese-speaking public. It had taken me ten whole months from the moment I first received the original copy of this book to the point when my efforts became a gigantic stack of translated drafts. The original text and the draft of my translation traveled halfway around the world with me as I was fortunate to be invited to visit *The New York Times* headquarters. These served as the reasons for my bothering many friends to ask for their advice and comment. Finally, after all of my exhaustion, struggles, and burning of the midnight oil, I can finally reap my reward.

Photo: Cover of Henry Ho's Chinese translation of *The Story of The New York Times* by Meyer Berger

This is a remarkable report written by an outstanding reporter. I marvel at this long, stirring tale told by a descriptive author who is exceptionally skilled at storytelling with anecdotes. For the ladies and gentlemen who read or publish the newspapers, this is an informative, interesting, and worthwhile read. It is a historical account that serves as a blueprint for how proper individual conduct combined with an archetype of corporate behavior, especially as applied to the newspaper industry, strives for and achieves success.

The year 1951 was the one-hundredth anniversary of the publication of *The New York Times.* To celebrate the achievements of its past century, the *Times* commissioned Meyer Berger, who dedicated his entire life to the newspaper, to compose this tremendous work. However, this is not a eulogistic, self-congratulatory book. Instead, it is a record of the success of a newspaper with behind-the-scenes accounts about many of the headline stories covered during its past one hundred years.

While I was perusing and translating the original text, I felt as if I were sitting next to the thundering printing machines, wandering through the hectic editorial department, and witnessing every major incident taking place in the past century, all while they were being covered, edited, typeset, printed, and peddled. Mr. Berger led me from the condemned building with window frames lacking windowpanes where the *Times* began, through years of hardship and strife to the *Times* becoming a prosperous leading newspaper empire. He introduced me to the people who founded *The New York Times* with courage and perseverance, to the people who endured all the hardships and made it great, to the people who traveled to all corners of the world to bring back the precious fruits of human endeavors, and to the people who shared these fruits with the world to be passed down forever.

The *Times'* efforts and accomplishments are substantial. It achieved corporate success in capital and asset growth. More importantly, it achieved many journalistic accolades, including winning the Pulitzer Prize twenty-four times over the thirty-three years from 1918 to 1951, including three team prizes. With a daily publishing run of more than 40,000,000 copies, its markets spread to every corner of the globe. The influence of its news reports and opinion commentaries is unsurpassed by any other newspaper in the world.

One hundred years, or a century, represents the largest practical measuring unit of time when considering the history of humanity. For a person, a hundred years of life would be a rare luxury through which to pass. One would be met with the sorrow of decrepitude even if one did manage to reach that milestone age. Take our respected late Mr. Dryfoos (publisher of the *Times* until 1963), who had conveyed his congratulations on the translation of this book, as an example. He passed away in early June of last year, and his duties were assumed by Arthur Hays Sulzberger's only son, Arthur Ochs Sulzberger. If a business has a history of a hundred years, it probably has soldiered through difficult periods from the starting line so that it may now stroll down easier paths. *The Story of The New York Times, 1851-1951* precisely bears witness for a successful business such as the *Times*.

(Translators' Note: Arthur Hays Sulzberger was publisher of The New York Times *from 1935 to 1961. He assumed this role when his father-in-law, Adolph Ochs, the previous* Times *publisher, died in 1935.)*

Over the one hundred years described in this book, editorials written in the *Times* numbered no fewer than 100,000, but only one was selected, copied word-for-word, and published in the appendix at the end of Berger's book. It has a special meaning for the Chinese people. The name of this commentary was "A Way of Life." It is dated the fifteenth of June 1938. It expounded on the sense of righteousness in Americans and all upstanding citizens of the world. It stated with certainty that "American opinion today is openly and overwhelmingly on the side of China against

Japan . . ." At the beginning of the second paragraph, the *Times* emphasized:

> In the case of China's fight for self-existence against Japanese aggression, American sentiment is tapped by loyalties which come readily to the surface. We cherish a special and long-standing friendship with the Chinese people. We resent the ruthlessness of Japan's attack . . . The American bankers and the American industrialists who dared to propose American participation in any plan to develop the resources of China under Japanese administration would find the opinion of this country overwhelmingly against him.

This editorial is very precious because it is timeless, especially in the wake of the menace of another global war – a war between freedom and tyranny, between capitalism and communism. The Cold War, a limited war, nuclear weapons, the space race – these are shrouding the world today with yet more pessimism in which all of mankind is at risk. Nevertheless, it is the impartial stance and conscientious voice of *The New York Times* that instills us with these beliefs:

- Although the world is fraught with evil and evil is pervasive, the truth never perishes.
- Kindness remains the essentiality of the majority.
- Righteousness remains the fountain of distinguishing right from wrong.

In times of chaos, despite the passage of twenty-five years, if steadfast American supporters of democracy remember what the *Times* stated, and the *Times* holds to its stance that "In any ultimate test of strength between democracy and dictatorship . . . we will be found on the side of those nations defending a way of life and the only way of life which Americans believe to be worth living," then we can remain optimistic within a gloomy world and have trust in our allies.

The Story of The New York Times, 1851-1951 provides journalists with a mirror of their profession to better appreciate the nobility and honor of their careers and to signal caution when framing stories as right or wrong because they hold the tools that influence and guide public opinion. To eliminate violence, to champion peace, to expose corruption and immorality in society, to report news of explorations of uncharted frozen territories over one hundred years, the *Times* has stood by its principles to be "impartial, independent, irrespective of distance or interest, reporting news justly and selflessly." No matter what dangers may exist to them individually or to the continued existence of the company, *Times* journalists have always fulfilled their obligation to the newspaper to be professionals who work according to such principles. For example, even if *Times* reporters obtain a piece of earth-shattering news, they may decide to lock it in the deepest drawer in the interests of safety, welfare for humanity, and the greater good.

The mere reader of newspapers will be just like me, learning undiscovered treasures of history and more from the many moving stories in *The Story of The New York Times, 1851-1951* and the multitude of news headlines during those one hundred years. More importantly, he will understand the purpose and true value of journalism. How do social phenomena become news through the talents and efforts of news reporters? How does the news develop motivational or restraining power? The answers to these questions, from my point of view, represent essential knowledge for modern-day citizens.

The free China of today is fortunate to have many outstanding and faithful journalists like those who are profiled in this book, as well as a populace that regards newspapers as intellectual sustenance. With all humility, I present and recommend this book to them.

(*Translators' Note: The term "free China" in 1964 was meant to describe Taiwan and not the People's Republic of China.*)

Strictly speaking, my experience and comprehension have not sufficiently prepared me to serve as the translator of this tome. Although I initially declined the kind offer from *Newsdom* [新聞天地] magazine's Chief Editor, Mr. Au Yeung Seun [歐陽醇], to tackle this project, it was the encouragement from his publisher, Mr. Pok Shau-fu [卜少夫], that I simply could not decline that provided the impetus for me to bravely take on this task. As Sulzberger stated, this story spanned over "a hapless hundred years." During that time, humanity experienced the catastrophe of the two World Wars and transitioned from the invention of the light bulb to the atomic age. In the past we regarded adventures to the uncharted North and South Poles as events that shocked the world. Now we have already rocketed to space and witnessed glimpses of the mysteries of the universe. Our ability to record and convey our experiences has jumped from words and photos in 2-D to film and television that portrays life in 3-

D. How many specific news events have this newspaper, which records the evolution and turmoil of humanity, accumulated?

This book also echoes *Newsdom's* motto: "The world is full of news, and in the news, there's the world." The scope of this book is incredibly vast. For that reason, my translation definitely goes beyond the simple conversion of words from English to Chinese. Thus, the obstacles faced by this translator are probably unfamiliar and unimaginable to the original author.

(Translators' Note: Newsdom *was a Chinese-language weekly magazine published in Hong Kong from 1945 to 2000 for which Henry Ho became a regular correspondent starting from the 1960s and into his later years.)*

Here are some examples of research that I conducted for this book. To better understand changes in the political climate of Italy, I once took the liberty to knock on the door and visit Mr. Liu Wen Tao [劉文島], the Chinese ambassador to Italy before the War of Resistance against Japan, on his sickbed. To correct the misnaming of an ancient Egyptian tomb, I wrote a letter to ask for assistance from Taipei's National History Museum. I even consulted the scholar, Mr. Tao Bai Chuan [陶百川], a fellow shipboard passenger who traveled with me across the Pacific Ocean. To answer my questions about natural science and social science, many friends or even people I barely knew became my teachers. Without a doubt, I spent much time determining how best to translate the many jargons used in journalism and the anecdotal idioms of New York City from one hundred years ago. Hopefully, readers will recognize my contributions to improving the understanding of the book, apart from simply translating its words, by reviewing the nearly two hundred translator's footnotes that I have added to this translation.

I am grateful for many things. I am thankful for: the honor of *Newsdom's* dedicating this book as part of its twentieth-anniversary celebration; the charismatic support from its publisher, Mr. Pok Shau-fu; its Chief Editor, Mr. Au Yeung Seun, a news enthusiast and a legendary journalist who discovered Berger's original text and served as the final proofreader for this Chinese translation; *The New York Times'* providing photographs and a biographical sketch of the author; the *Times'* earnestness in inviting me to visit their headquarters; my good friends Mr. and Mrs. Pauley, Mr. Wong Gee Wen [王季文], and all the aforementioned people who provided advice for this translation; and my dear wife, Peggy, who not only helped me with copying manuscripts but also shouldered the burden of taking care of our family, thereby allowing me time to commit to the avocation about which I am passionate – the translation of important texts. The Chinese version of this text would not exist if it were not for the help of these individuals. Let me express my sincerest gratitude.

Last year, on the second of August, when *The New York Times* published the news of my translation of this book, its Chairman of the Board, Mr. Arthur Hays Sulzberger, immediately penned a congratulatory letter to me through the Munson Institute for American Maritime History in Mystic, Connecticut, where I was a visiting researcher. He wrote, "I am indeed deeply impressed by what I read in *The New York Times* about your translating the Meyer Berger story into Chinese. I sincerely hope your efforts will be appreciated and remunerative."

Photo: Letter of appreciation from *The New York Times* Chairman of the Board Arthur Hays Sulzberger

At the time, my friends and fellow researchers attending the Maritime History Symposium at Mystic thought this was a rare honor, but I should rather share this honor with the many people who made a concerted effort at helping me to translate this extensive work.

As a customary habit, I would like to make a statement here. The original book is like a faultless piece of jade, whereas this Chinese translation is at best a replica. Not only is it not on par with the original, but there inevitably will be some mistakes. To my fellow readers, please do not hesitate to convey how my translation may be corrected. In the meantime, please believe that I have tried my very best.

Henry Yu-Heng Ho
Taoyuan [濤園] Navy Dormitory, Taipei, Christmas Eve, 1964

Photo: Henry Ho conducting research for his translation at the headquarters office of *The New York Times* circa 1963

United States: 1965 to 1988

12

Repressed Tears of Chinese Students in America

An Aerogram from Los Angeles

by Henry Yu-Heng Ho
from *Newsdom,* 1964
as part of his Monthly Journal Series (摘月記續篇)

Publisher's Preface: The writer of this article is currently visiting America. He began and continues to dispatch to us his observations while traveling under this "Monthly Journal" series. In this dispatch from Los Angeles, he describes the bitter hardships in the lives of the graduate students from Taiwan who are studying in this American "paradise." It is our hope that this essay proves to be a useful reference for young people who are about to depart for their journeys to America.

*****

America is considered by many to be a utopia from the perspective of material enjoyment and as a land of opportunity. In today's troubled world, America can be considered a paradise. Yet during my visit here, I saw streaks of tears on the faces of many of our fellow students.

First, A Few Statements

This is not sensational fiction, but a true account of what I've seen and heard. Before I proceed, I should make the following statements:

1. The Chinese students in this paradise are not entirely without joy. Who hasn't read those eye-catching joyous wedding announcements frequently found in our newspapers? "We would like to formally announce the engagement of the number three son from the Zhang family to the number four daughter from the Li family. They are to be married in Anytown, U.S.A. at some church." Seeing this in print makes the announcer proud and the readers envious. Who hasn't heard about certain individuals who have earned their Ph.D. or heard news that someone has newly invented something while abroad that brings glory to the nation? Who doesn't know someone who boasts openly and often about how comfortable and wealthy his or her relatives who live abroad are? Who doesn't know someone who is constantly relating how hard his or her relative abroad studies? This is but one aspect of the lives of Chinese students living in this paradise called America – a garden where sweet fruit grows from magnificent flowers nourished by the bitter tears from our students. Moreover, they put on smiling faces after the streaks of their tears have been wiped away. But conveying this type of cheerful but superficial news is not part of my dispatch.

2. I am neither an official investigator nor an "envoy of comfort." It's just that these students are either directly or indirectly my friends. They have given me many opportunities, ranging from discussions, visits, having dinner together, staying with them even overnight, and even observing actual situations as a bystander, to see, to hear, and to be moved by their misery. Thus, I have concealed their actual names, but readers please believe that my accounts about them are true.

3. I wish not to reveal anyone's shortcomings. On the contrary, by covering aspects of their lives that my compatriots themselves often do not talk about, I now have a deeper understanding and

admiration for them. This has also created in me an infectious sympathy. If I am able to contribute to the beginning of a better understanding for students or family members preparing to, or those with the ambition to, come to the U.S., that would be an unexpected bonus.
4. This article does not include the experiences of our female students in America as I had not visited their dormitory rooms or had an opportunity to listen to their confidences.

What Is the Price for Precious Laurel?

Studying abroad is a glorious event for both the student and his or her family. It requires years of arduous preparation starting as early as kindergarten and culminating with securing an American student visa from the local U.S. embassy. The lengthy process is consummated only through the collective effort of all parties involved. As our ship cast off her lines for the long voyage to America, I stood as a bystander and watched the students onboard wave long goodbyes to family and friends ashore. At that moment, I began to understand their mixed emotions. On the one hand, they are sad and apprehensive to depart on an odyssey not knowing when they might see their loved ones from the Old World again. On the other hand, both they and their parents are joyously celebrating the spreading of their wings to soar higher and to a better place. What's more, in the eyes of our countrymen, "studying abroad" is a precious laurel that symbolizes the bright future and fortunes waiting ahead.

(Translators' Note: Due to the expense of air travel in the 1950s and 1960s, most self-funded scholars on student visas made the long journey by ship from Taiwan to the U.S. For many students, it was not their intent to return to Taiwan, but to finish their studies, find a job, get married, and settle down in the U.S.)

The modern-day post-graduate studies can be categorized into the areas of science, engineering, and liberal arts. The pursuit of these different fields should be based on one's interests. However, with America emphasizing industrial development after World War II and seeking to excel both in commercial and defense industries, an enormous amount of money from her defense organizations, manufacturing companies, government, and private enterprises is being poured into American universities. These stakeholders encourage professors and their students to perform research in the areas that are most relevant to their respective interests. Because of this, scholarships, teaching assistantships, and research grants in the fields of science and engineering are easier to realize. Likewise, jobs in laboratories and factories are easier to find. Since scientists and engineers communicate through numbers and symbols, foreign students who are inherently deficient in both English and awareness of cultural norms will encounter fewer academic challenges by studying in the engineering and scientific disciplines.

(Translators' Note: The general strategy of self-funded students in question was to arrive in America with enough cash to pay for one year of tuition and living costs. After that, they hoped to obtain scholarship support. If not, they could always work in a Chinese restaurant "under the table.")

Chinese students who study literature or law in America have fewer opportunities to receive scholarships as their English comprehension and communication skills are naturally handicapped compared with their peers who are born and raised in America. Since they also arrive with less of an academic reputation and network, they have fewer chances to obtain scholarships or to enroll in part-time jobs related to their field of study. Some students had to settle for less desirable ways to live, thus had to subsidize their living and tuition costs through low-wage jobs that often involved working in a harsher environment.

Serving the Sick and Delivering the Dead

In America, it is common for students to work in order to support their educational expenses. A student who works [打工], irrespective of whatever type of job he or she holds, will not be regarded as an embarrassment by others, unlike in Asia. As we know, some Chinese students who wash dishes or work in the kitchen or wait tables in a summer resort have earned an entire year of tuition in two or three months. Mr. Peng Ge's [彭歌] novel *At the Edge of Heaven* [在天之涯] provides a lifelike portrayal of such students. To supplement Mr. Peng's book, here are two special cases when our Chinese students could not find this type of summer resort job.

(Translators' Note: Working at summer resorts had the added benefit to students of the employer's providing food and lodging.)

Working as an attendant at a nursing home: Someone once said, "America is heaven for the young, a workplace for the middle-aged, and hell for the elderly." Although this saying may be an exaggeration, the custom here is to abandon the elderly. After spending a lifetime enslaved like oxen and horses for the sake of their children, they despondently enter nursing homes in their twilight years. Many of them suffer constipation and are bedridden. Although caring for one's elderly parent is a part of the duties of filial piety, working in a nursing home remains an option, though less desirable, when other part-time jobs are not available. But at least it is an opportunity to earn wages.

Working in a hospital morgue: A hospital in a city once advertised for an orderly whose job it would be to move deceased patients to the morgue and then wheel the frozen bodies into the hands of funeral home staff when they arrived for the transfer. Soon after this want ad came out, one brave student quickly answered and was hired for this unique job.

Regardless of the type of work, American employers calculate the expected workload very precisely and simply do not pay for someone to sit around. After one day of manual labor, you can imagine the physical exhaustion for these students.

Midnight Tears Soak Pillowcases

Isolation and loneliness gnaw at every foreign student's heart. Perhaps they also eat away at the hearts of everyone who journeys abroad. For foreign students at many universities, two or three Chinese students sharing a single living quarters is a common practice to save money. Since they have different class and work schedules, there is very little time to socialize with one another. The phrase "having nothing to do" does not exist for Chinese students in America, so there is little time to engage in gossip. But when our students lie awake deep at night, they have much to think about. They think about how far away they are from home. They think about their own struggles. They think about how much they miss their home and the land of their birth. They think about the messy world we live in. Thus, it is not surprising that their pillows are soaked with tears.

During the Dragon Boat Festival [端午節] this year, I was unexpectedly pulled by my friend to attend a dinner at an apartment in Los Angeles. There, seven or eight male students sat around a round dinner table enjoying festival dishes such as soy sauce-braised fish and pork. There were also homemade zongzi [粽子] typically served during this important Chinese holiday. Although their zongzi-wrapping skills were nowhere near those of our loving mothers and sisters back home, they had gone all the way to Chinatown to purchase glutinous rice and bamboo

leaves to celebrate this holiday just as if they were at home. That they did this reflects clearly their yearning for their home and the Old Country.
(Translators' Note: Zongzi are glutinous rice dumplings stuffed with different fillings and wrapped in bamboo leaves.)

Marriage is a stressful matter for our students. Especially on an American campus where our students struggle seeing liberal sexual behaviors that contrast with their own conservative upbringings. Such struggles can keep them up at night and even result in melancholy. Other than for a few lucky individuals, romance and having a love life often become pursuits that are out of bounds for our students, who may be emotionally shackled to a sweetheart left behind. The possibility of Sino-American marriages is extremely low. As well, there are far fewer women than men as Chinese students in America. Also, the few female students who are able to study abroad often are focused more on their professional goals and trying to meet their own high expectations. They are either too busy striving for their master's or Ph.D. degrees or have set their goal for a sweetheart to be a "doctorate-level" man of excellence. While there are more Ph.D.'s in America than back home, such an academic honor is still not an easy thing to earn. As they see their younger years fleeting away, many students may slowly fade into gloomy corners. While they may have achieved academic prominence and success, they may also have wasted the sweetest years of their lives. It is no wonder that some are promoting the idea of "exporting brides" from the home country. But some of our students in America have only a limited-stay visa tied with their programs of study. What, then, would a bride from the motherland have to rely on when that visa is no longer?

Hearts Tied to Homeland

The weekly editorial published in the 852nd issue of *Newsdom*, titled "Exchange Students Having Trouble [留美學生出問題]," highlighted some facts that deserve soul searching. The so-called "earn some money first and study later" thinking is not a fabrication. Such an attitude does cause anxiety for our students in America. They are not greedy to procure American citizenship. However, anyone who works hard in this economically thriving and politically stable environment will be materially rewarded better than in one's home country. This opportunity is a real temptation for our young people in America.

Deep down our students remain highly educated individuals who still dream of building a beautiful future with scholarly self-respect. Cast adrift within American society as an outsider, they develop a stronger sense of patriotism to the motherland. One is sympathetic to their struggles as their paths in America appear to be more challenging than those of the previous generation of Chinese who came to this "land of the gold." Many of the earlier generation spent years washing laundry, cooking "chop-suey" at restaurants, and living thriftily. After some years they were able to raise a family before returning to their home country in glory. However, mainland China has undergone significant change politically, economically, and socially, while Hong Kong and Taiwan remain overcrowded. Some of our mainland-born students in America also consider Hong Kong and Taiwan as places to visit, but not necessarily a home country to which to return. Even those with no family ties to either Hong Kong or Taiwan are questioning themselves as to where they should return.

America is not "heaven on earth" for every one of our students. Influenced by various factors in this "heaven," our students become drifters without a home to return to. Even though they can earn an income several times higher and are envied by others at home, the higher costs of living in America may not result in a comparable quality of life. I daresay they are all praying, hoping, and waiting for the day their homeland becomes stronger so that it may afford them the opportunity to demonstrate their skills. When that time comes, they will certainly end this nomadic life, throw away the comfortable salary, and voluntarily return home. After all, they are university students! Masters! Doctorates! After all, they are all Chinese!

13

I Am a Nurse

by Peggy Ho
An Award-Winning Essay from Taiwan's
The Rambler magazine (自由談), 1962

The January 1957 volume of *American Nurses Monthly* magazine published a letter from a well-known Captain in the United States Marine Corps titled "I Don't Want My Wife to Be a Nurse." In this letter he said, with a hint of anger, "It's not that I object to her working. I also admit that going to work can provide greater fulfillment than spending all day at home as a housewife. I'm even more proud she's in a profession so well-respected by others. After twenty years in the military, the time I've spent in hospitals as an admitted patient has been enough for me to understand what a nurse's job entails. I'm quite familiar with their arduous and important responsibilities. It's precisely because of my respect that I was motivated to write this letter . . . even in today's California, there are dozens of doctors who have retired as millionaires – but what about nurses? It would be better if she puts away the ideals and sense of glory bestowed on newly crowned nurses during the golden days because even with working overtime it's difficult to make a living as she is paid (at the discretion of a private doctor) at a level less than a chauffeur or waitress . . ."

In the same issue, the magazine published a reply from the American Nurses Society: " . . . nurses have united to strive for improvements to employment conditions. They have already won better treatment at work and a new kind of respect. As a result, nurses who are dedicated to their careers are able to provide patients with proper care. . . . A nurse who has devoted herself to her profession with the idealistic goal to serve others should be considered a part of our democracy. Like other successes in a democratic society, this can only be accomplished by those with courage and willingness to work hard together . . ."

These two perspectives show the two faces of nursing – bitter and happy, light and dark. In particular, the terms "courage and willingness" seem to be the most appropriate words to describe my more than ten years as a nurse.

I

When I was accepted into nursing school, Father indirectly remarked that he was afraid I would not graduate. As he was a father who otherwise always encouraged and praised his children, I've always remembered clearly his words. I do not know if this was his being realistic or possibly a method to motivate me.

Indeed I have often been called timid. I'm most afraid of running into danger and injury. Seeing blood made me feel helpless, earning taunts from my siblings. For this reason, I should have stayed far, far away from situations that would expose me to diseases and sickness, and instead study something like education, art, music, or some other field more suitable to my personality. It was just that when I was small, I was once admitted to the hospital. Seeing the young female nurses and the way their well-starched snow-white uniforms rustled with soft crackling sounds as they moved busily and took care of patients, as well as their capability and skill to lessen patients' suffering (which moved me at the time), was deeply ingrained in my mind, thereby encouraging me to set foot in nursing school.

My nursing school days were certainly a challenge and torment. The first time I held a human skull, to learn and remember the names of the bones, my hands trembled. I didn't dare look directly into those frightening empty eye sockets. But as with many other things, I still gathered my courage and did it. Even on the eve of a big exam, I borrowed a skull and placed it next to my pillow, touching it to memorize all of its parts until late at night. That night I fell asleep under the gaze of that skull with its empty eyes and clenched teeth.

On the night of our candlelit graduation ceremony, students dressed in white filled the school's auditorium. In the flickering candlelight, I was excited because of the solemn and sacred atmosphere. The entire ceremony evoked the ideal of the paragon Florence Nightingale as we took responsibility for the honor of joining the nursing profession. Yet from then on, I rarely thought about it again. Stepping into a society of graduates that brought me into contact with the larger community of nursing professionals, I gradually realized I represented more than just myself; rather, I was in only a small ring in a much larger society. The nursing profession is not purely to serve others; it is also for one's self. Naturally, I can also honestly say I have no complaints about my profession. I think, for a woman, nursing is a good profession. What we learn has practical applications for society, family, and the individual.

II

I regard nursing as not just a job as I can approach it with a sense of self-amusement and humor. Humans have no way to cast off the torment of illness. I daresay nurses can help people feel the treasure of good health and the true good fortune of being without illness.

In the hospital, the relationship between doctors and patients is not nearly as intimate as that with the nurse. The former, after touring the ward once or twice a day, give orders and then leave, whereas, during an eight-hour shift, nurses are inseparable from their patients, attending to the minute details of their lives. Though nurses are considered "angels in white," some patients don't entirely understand the duties of the nursing profession and don't completely know that nurses are driven by a sense of responsibility or sympathy, doing their best to alleviate patients' suffering and to hasten an early recovery. Those who are ill are often emotionally flustered. Those who think themselves to be unlucky would often make excessive demands of nurses. For example, some patients criticize nurses who fail to meet their expectations with exaggerated complaints about their poor attitudes, but perhaps they should consider that nurses work year in and year out in the company of disease, pain, and the groaning of the ill. Sometimes it can influence a person's state of mind. Of course, I am not partial to those nurses who are fiendish to patients all day. I feel that although nurses are honored as "angels in white," in the end they are also only human. Yet no matter what, when a patient leaves the hospital with good health and a smile, this is always a happy thing for his or her nurse.

Even in the same hospital, the moods within different wards are not completely the same. Surgery patients can arrive from the Emergency Department with mangled and broken limbs or as an otherwise normal-appearing person who in several days will have their abdomens opened, but at some point, they all will have the same moans and wails. However, when you see them bounce back from the brink of death, you have to be amazed by the miracle of the tenacious human body and the god-like effects of modern medicine.

The atmosphere around the internal medicine patients is mostly silent and relatively unchanging. Here there is less drama than in the surgical wards. Some beds are occupied by elderly patients for long periods. The graphs on their patient charts rarely have many ups and downs. The same sad faces, the same listless and dispirited expressions that cast a shadow over those lingering in their sickbeds made one's mood heavy.

The operating rooms seem to be the place most devoid of emotion. All day we count and wipe those surgical instruments glistening like snow in the sun. All day we wrap ourselves in rubber aprons while cleaning and removing bloodstains and amputated limbs. All day our bodies are covered and hidden except for a pair of eyes. We stare at those disinfected sheets and towels that cover the patient except for the area where the incision is to be made – patients are represented only by that square of exposed skin awaiting the knife.

I like the pediatric ward the most. It would seem like these young seedlings would be the weakest, but in reality, their childish innocence makes them the strongest. When children feel sick, it's even more revealing. Similarly when they are tormented by illness, they rarely have a fear of death. Through them, one can easily comprehend the value of continuing to live and the meaning behind our work.

Some deaths hit particularly hard making one especially sad. I remember my first night shift as a new graduate. There was a dying patient. We used every possible means to save him. The only thing left was to wait for God to call him home. He had been an inpatient for two weeks. He was a neglected, lonely man with few friends, maybe because of life's adversities. He was always submissive, polite but with a corresponding sense of inferiority. In the silent patient ward, I gazed at the screen obstructing the view of Bed 13. Every so often I would tiptoe to sneak a peek at him. At about 2 a.m., he opened his eyes as if he had been waiting for me to come.

He smiled at me, asking hoarsely, "Am I going to die?" He wore a beseeching expression.

"You'll get better," I quietly replied, fluffing his pillow for him. He didn't believe me but wanted to be polite. The muscles of his face trembled a little. In the faint light, I could make out a mournful but barely expressed bitter smile.

"Miss, could you sit here for a moment? I'm feeling very lonely." I wanted to cry. I wanted to go far, far away, but I knew I could not show him those emotions as I would cause him more suffering.

The patient's breathing and pulse grew even weaker. I had to go inform the doctor. As I moved to leave, he opened wide both eyes as if to beg, "Please don't leave." I scrambled, running to the end of the long corridor to grab the phone.

Even though the doctor came, he didn't wait for me to draw the epinephrine from the medicine bottle. The patient had already breathed his last breath. That was the first time I saw a life end, making me sad for some time.

This reminds me of a little boy named Mike. He was one of my congenital heart patients at the Cincinnati Children's Hospital who was awaiting heart surgery. The doctor had already explained very clearly to his parents that the prognosis for his surgery was 50 percent for survival and 50 percent for death. He was admitted as an inpatient to strengthen his body in preparation for surgery. In America – a "children's paradise" – a young sprout with no way to grow up seemed a particularly pitiful and cruel twist of fate to me. Perhaps it was God's will. He looked particularly cute, and we became good friends. He knew I came from faraway China and begged me to tell him stories about China. Because I gave him a Christmas card printed with children setting off fireworks, he innocently requested that after he got better, I bring him to China and also buy a large amount of fireworks for him to play with. I promised him I would – of course, this was a heart-breaking promise that I knew could not be fulfilled.

Day after day Mike put on a smile, waiting for me to start work. I always think about him. It's just that when his extremely shortened life came to an end, I wasn't there. It happened during the Chinese Lunar New Year. I had gone to Chicago for a visit. Mike remembered that I once had told him that Chinese New Year was the very time Chinese children would merrily set off fireworks. When I returned from my trip a coworker related that Mike had gone to the operating room telling her, "Peggy said she would bring me to China. We're going to buy a boatload of fireworks to bring back."

I cried then, cried with such grief, perhaps complicated by the feeling of drifting aimlessly as a guest in a foreign land. I went to his grave, brushing away the accumulated snow to place some fresh flowers, and tearfully and reluctantly told him, "Mike, I'm going back to China. Come with me. We'll go buy a boatload of fireworks."

Photo: Peggy Ho as a foreign exchange nurse at Cincinnati Children's Hospital in the late 1950s

III

I am not intentionally advocating for the nursing profession, but nursing's progress toward science, professionalism, and its institutionalization, even in the U.S., has only occurred over the past thirty years. Yet in our society many unreasonable, misunderstood, and indifferent attitudes about nursing still clearly exist.

A few years ago a doctor put out an advertisement (whether he was in private practice I wasn't able to find out) to recruit a nurse. The conditions were that she must be able to endure hardship, as well as to cook and to raise children. . . . Not long before, our local newspaper reported about a well-known female celebrity who put on an "angel in white" uniform. Just with that, she began working as a nurse in her husband's clinic. One cannot fault a woman's sense of duty to support her husband. However, if there truly exists a shortcut to allow one in no time to become a qualified and experienced nurse, then it would seem there is no need for the rigorous and seemingly endless nursing education. Besides, the nursing license required under national laws would then become wastepaper. One cannot blame the newspaper reporter for praising her as he does not know the details of the required training and licensure for nurses. What we nurses could not understand, however, was how a well-respected general practitioner could ignore the requirements of his profession. This story brings shame to nursing. If I were a doctor, I would rather invite an ordinary, but experienced nurse to give an injection, because my purpose is to cure. Beauty and fame are not necessary for nursing. They have no use in helping patients recover.

*****

When I graduated, a relative once asked, half-flatteringly and half-curiously, "Now that you've graduated, how long will you be at the hospital before you can be a doctor?"

Nurses are nurses; doctors are doctors. Both professions cooperate closely. The doctor and the nurse travel different paths but work toward the same goal – that is, to lessen the pain that can be found in human living, aging, sickness, and death.

14

A Chinese Family in America

by Henry Yu-Heng Ho
from issue No. 1313 of *Newsdom*,
April 13, 1974

Translators' Note: Below is an excerpt from an annual letter for 1973 that our father would write to friends and family relating the notable events and developments of the past year. Several of these were published in magazines such as Newsdom *as a means to inform the general populace in Taiwan and Hong Kong of what life in the United States was like.*

Publisher Pok Shau-fu's Preface:

This article was authored by our correspondent in New York City. Although originally written as a private letter that relates family matters, it helps our readers to understand the life of a Chinese family in America as well as their views of the New World.

*****

Dear xx:

. . . The most noteworthy event to report from last year was not our vacation to the famous Yellowstone National Park, but rather our "modern" means of transport during the vacation. Three seafarers and their families, including ours, all from the New York City area, decided on a whim to vacation together in a rented mobile home. Twelve of us crammed together into one vehicle. We divided the long drive into three shifts, similar to that of round-the-clock ship's watches, as we drove 2,200 miles to our destination in the western wilderness.

Do not belittle this ten-wheeled vehicle that we called "home" for the duration of our trip. It was fully equipped with three double beds plus one single bed. It also had an eating area, bathroom, shower, air conditioner and heater, stove and oven, refrigerator and sinks, washbasin, closets for clothing, cooking wares, hot water heater, and drainage for sewage and waste. All we needed to eat, drink, relieve ourselves, and sleep were inside a single home on wheels. It is hard to fathom that one can stuff all of these facilities into one vehicle, but I do not boast here.

Photo: Three families that crowded into a Winnebago mobile home and journeyed to national parks during the summer of 1973

We visited Yellowstone National Park, which was formed after the Ice Age and further shaped by periods of volcanic activity thousands of years ago. We next toured Grand Teton National Park, which was as beautiful as Switzerland. On the way back to the East Coast, we drove to Canada by way of Detroit. We stopped at Toronto's Chinatown before going on to what we jokingly called "the Big-Broken-Rag-in-Your-House," [你家那塊大破布] which is also called Niagara Falls, before finally returning to New York City.

(Translators' Note: "Big-Broken-Rag-in-Your-House" is a direct phonetic English to Chinese translation of Niagara Falls. The all-in cost for this fourteen-day trip that covered over 4,500 miles of driving was carefully recorded by the three mothers onboard and totaled only $2,866.)

While we enjoyed the trip, the means by which we traveled was more memorable to us. Ironically, such a style of travel also matches our daily lifestyle in America, which is characterized by a "Rush! Rush! Rush!" mentality. Although we covered a large area of the country in a brief two-week period, still we were able to try many activities such as whitewater rafting, horseback riding, sailing, cooking over a campfire, swimming, fishing, and hiking. We had time to make our own sandwiches as well as eat at some gourmet restaurants. It seemed that we completed all possible fun-filled activities for the year in one fell swoop. I plan to publish a detailed travel journey later as I already have a draft in my mind, but not a deadline for doing so . .

Photo: Henry, Peggy and Peter Ho at Grand Teton National Park, Wyoming

As for our daily life at home, there is nothing new to report except that we bought a freezer to hedge against the current crisis in meat prices. Peggy then purchased half of a cow, yes literally, to fill the new freezer. It seemed to be a fairytale thing to do. At the local wholesale butcher shop, our half of a cow was sawed and cut into many different kinds of steaks, stew meat cubes, barbecue slices, shanks, and even soup bones. Each portion of meat came carefully wrapped; some were stored frozen at the shop as we could not take all of it home. After making two more trips back to the butcher shop to collect what is ours, we are about to finish this half-cow. While we never estimated how much money we saved, we did enjoy the convenience of this bounty of beef at home.

Not Forgetting Our Chinese

If you ever visited our home, you would have noticed a table of fines posted on the kitchen wall. The fines were levied in categories of one dollar, one quarter, one nickel, and one penny. For each category, its score is tallied by using the Chinese character of 正 to represent every five violations committed. This is part of our new house rule – a fine for each time an English sentence is spoken at the dinner table. One dollar for Henry, one quarter for Peggy, one nickel for David, and one penny for Peter. To date the one-dollar fine was assessed eight times, the quarter fine nine times, the nickel fine eight times, and the penny fine tallied a total of thirty-seven times! This rule was designed to help Peter to remember and to use his Chinese. So far it seems to be working.

However, when Peter is anxious and unable to make a point in Chinese, he will quickly move behind his chair and speak in English. He has interpreted that this rule applies only when one is actually "sitting down" at the dinner table. Therefore, his speaking English while "standing up" at the table is excluded from being assessed a fine. Since our legislation did not adequately cover this exception, we have no choice but to let him go on this loophole.

At Christmas, we bought a ping-pong table as a house gift and placed it in the basement. This popular gift helped everyone to share a common hobby and was partly financed by our collection of dinner-table fines.

America's Strength and Weakness

The winter of 1972 was unseasonably warm. I recall only two snow shoveling days. Because of fewer snow days, New York City was able to save $5 million in expenses for snow removal and salt (which helps to melt the snow on her streets). From this figure, one can appreciate the size of New York City. Or else, the value of the U.S. dollar is depreciating. The weak American dollar plus the ongoing rise in food prices (especially for meat) has resulted in plenty of criticisms from within America and around the world.

From the Korean War to the Vietnam War, America's military might was ingloriously tested and has disappointed her allies. The weakening of the dollar has exposed her economic problems. However, some still have faith in her potential as she has plenty of land, resources, and people. As a common citizen, I am unable to make heads or tails about this, but these are certainly turbulent times in our history. Anyway, these worldly issues are beyond our consideration as none of us has the burden of being the President!

Other Matters to Report

Peter has graduated from sixth grade and has started in our local junior high school. It is located closer to our home in Fort Lee and is an easy downhill walk for him. He is hooked on playing chess. He will read the book *Bobby Fisher Teaches Chess* every night before going to sleep. He plays against his older brother and sometimes manages a draw.

David is in his third year in college. He has lots of homework and continues to play tennis. With his university campus in Manhattan he has come to know a lot about New York City and can be a good guide when you visit us. Peggy is very successful at home horticulture. Her green plants in the atrium room lighten the gray and depressing winter days. Henry enjoys swimming as his exercise. He has been swimming over a year and gradually over time has increased the distance to one mile. He now also excels at home repair skills such as repairing water pipes and heaters. He has purchased plenty of tools and is sometimes invited by friends tens of miles away to fix their house problems.

I had planned for the family to visit Taiwan this summer; however, looking at various other schedules, it looks like we will delay the visit for one year . . .

Sincerely,

Henry & Peggy, 1973

15

From Captain to Bricklayer
A Year-End Letter from Henry Ho to All His Caring Friends

by Henry Yu-Heng Ho
from *Newsdom*, 1989

Translators' Note: As noted in Mr. Pok's introductory commentary below, this letter was part of a series of annual communiqués authored at the end of each year by our father. This is the last one of many written over a span of at least three decades. Within ten months from completing this letter for 1988, Henry Ho would develop neurological symptoms that would prevent him from drafting his annual letter for 1989. After a series of misdiagnoses, he was ultimately diagnosed with a very rare and uniformly fatal neurodegenerative disorder that would prematurely take him from us in October of 1990, less than two years after this letter was shared with friends and family. As such, this letter has a special meaning for us.

Publisher Pok Shau-fu's Preface:

Henry Ho served in the Navy as Captain of several naval vessels. After retirement from the Navy, he joined the merchant marine industry. He also served as a Captain of merchant vessels and subsequently as a shore-based Port Captain. He is an old friend and a frequent contributor to *Newsdom* magazine. He is an author who has also translated *The Story of the New York Times: 1851-1951,* which was published by *Newsdom*. At the end of each year, he writes a letter to his friends sharing stories about his life and family highlights. Below is this year's [1988] letter. He no longer works in the maritime industry and has yet to decide what he will be doing in the next year. In this letter, "Peggy" is his wife while "David" and "Peter" are his sons.

*****

Dear xx:

The blazing mid-November sun shone through the southern window, making my small study room feel bright and warm like spring. Outside my window, a few stubborn yellow leaves withered on the oak tree branches as two squirrels were busy picking up acorns in their mouths before burying them in the ground for the winter. The scenery and mood reflect a portrait of our lives.

The shipping business has suffered setbacks and continues to be weak. Many large companies are tightening their belts while smaller ones are unable to survive by themselves. I have no reason to hang around in this industry, which in the past consistently provided for my family. Upon my retirement, we moved from Connecticut back to New Jersey. Although I am not ready to rock away my remaining life on a chair, as they say in the West, I also am not expecting anyone to invite me to un-retire. So, I decided it is time to do some of the things I can do and like to do. First, I thought about writing a memoir of my life similar to the essay series "Hair, Navy and Me," published several years ago. Many of my stories of life on the seas should attract reader interest. But other things have intervened and so I have yet to pick up my "amateur scribbler's" pen again.

Building My Own House

You may recall from our past annual letters that I frequently mentioned house care and maintenance as a hobby. Since we immigrated to America in 1966 and purchased our first home in 1968, which I named the Westview Cottage (previously owned), we have since lived in the White Stone House (newly built), Henry's Morning Mansion (newly built), South Street Old House (historical building that we rented), and Forever Sea Mansion (newly built). I gradually accumulated know-how through lessons learned and watching how others take care of their own homes. Upon our move back to New Jersey, my nephew Raymond Tong (son of Professor TeKong Tong [唐德剛]), who is an architecture graduate of Columbia University, provided design and contracting assistance to me for a major teardown and rebuild of an older home to meet our liking.

Photo: Henry and Peggy Ho during the demolition phase of house rebuilding in Fort Lee, NJ

We submitted architectural drawings in February for approval by the town and started work in April with the goal to move in by mid-December. I took on the role of general contractor by myself. Every day, rain or shine, I visited the site early in the morning and returned home late at night. There was plenty of work in arranging subcontractors, site inspections, purchasing materials, and coordinating work at the construction site. My wife and I were busy, but we felt happy. Learning as I went along, the days flew by quickly and the house is now nearing completion. Neighbors say it is the "prettiest" house on the block; some even called it "an architect's home" (i.e., a work of art) as it is quite different than a commercially built home. I would like to share with you my experience and impressions.

To build a home in America, one does not necessarily need to possess professional knowledge, but you should have a broad and common understanding of construction plus some skill to arrange work in an orderly manner. Also, when dealing with contractors, it is helpful to know when to be tough and when to let up. Of course, developing a trusting and fair relationship with others is also helpful.

In America blue-collar worker wages are rising steadily. In the past, a project's labor and material costs each were about half of the total. Now the labor portion is about three times that of materials. Some subcontractors will only quote labor costs and leave material sourcing to others. Some are not interested in doing a "small job" like ours. When they are busy, they quote sky-high prices. For example, the going labor rate for tile workers is about $5 per square foot for tile, $8 for marble, and $14 for granite. The rest you can deduce.

Photo: Fort Lee house construction. The original house was single story.

On other housing matters, American homes change rapidly with new building materials and construction methods, which are constantly being introduced to suit different individual tastes. The current trend is to avoid square-shaped homes in both exterior and interior dimensions. New houses are being furnished with a variety of different window and door types and sizes. Kitchens and bathrooms are getting larger and larger and are being fitted with the latest appliances and fittings. A house without a whirlpool tub and steam shower would be considered an inferior-class dwelling. Brick houses are already thought of as factory-like buildings, lacking in artistic form and style. Everyone loves to let in sunlight or have bright lights in their home. Some houses are equipped with computer-controlled curtains, roof-mounted skylights, and even room lights that can also be turned on and off electronically. Americans are not particular about what they wear or eat, but they often spare no cost on houses since they are considered a good investment.

Although ours was a stand-alone house that was rebuilt, the construction methods we used were similar to those of an industrial assembly line. The project is finely subdivided according to each subcontractor's specialties because they each use their own special tools. Let me count the various subcontractors involved with our project according to the sequence of their work: site excavation and formation; concrete foundation; wood frame erection; roofing; electrical; pipe and heating; central air-conditioning; audio system; anti-theft alarms; fire-proofing; telephone; TV system; intercom and central vacuum system; gutter and drains; sound and heat insulation; carpeting; tiling and flooring; painting; and finally the exterior landscaping.

Photo: Completion of the house on Abbott Blvd., January 1989

Family Highlights

Other than learning how to build a house, I have taught myself how to make tasty homemade bran bread and steamed Chinese mantous [steamed buns]. It seems my friends appreciate my efforts to the point that my supply couldn't meet their demand. Perhaps it is due to my being homesick or nostalgic that my original Chinese mantous taste better than all other bakery treats in this country. At the same time, mine do not have any preservatives, so it is healthier than any other food.

Peggy continues to work at the hospital on a schedule of four days on and ten days off. Her job also helps her to keep up with the ever-changing science of medicine. After answering a New York City Chinatown newspaper's call for volunteers to help the elderly whose children are living far away, she visits them in Chinatown from time to time. One day her hospital informed her that their computer had miscalculated her salary and that they were very sorry for their error. Peggy calmly told them, "You know I have never known how much money I make. Every time I get paid, my salary is deposited directly into a special savings account for my grandchildren's tuitions." The woman repeatedly praised her and said, "I wish I had a grandmother like that."

David is still working in Beijing with GE. He's well versed in China's current affairs. He has an honest and kind character. Many people there know him and have a pretty good impression of him. Although we are living in the U.S., we have entertained on his behalf many of his Chinese friends who visited the States. He and our granddaughters will be visiting us in the upcoming months. I am in the middle of preparing for them to stay with us in this new house.

Peter is still studying at Yale Medical School. Our daughter-in-law, Hui Ping, is working on her master's degree at Columbia University and is living with us. This October one of Peter's medical articles was published in the *Yale Alumni Magazine*. The article was translated by our dear friend Guan-Yu and was published in Taiwan's *Union Daily*. I attach a copy for sharing.

You may want to ask the address of our new home. It is 1222 Abbott Blvd., Fort Lee, NJ. If you do not wish to remember this new address, you can always post letters to us at the White Stone House in Englewood Cliffs.

If you are in New York, we welcome you to tour this amateur's masterpiece.

What will I be doing next year? Even I do not know. This is because: 1) I am kicking my feet up. Whatever I like to do or want to do, I will do; 2) A friend who knows me well made the following observation, saying, "You really are a jack of all trades." Indeed, I have studied in England, served in the Navy, done farming, worked in both industrial and commercial businesses. I have tried everything, and even though I don't have any significant accomplishments, I have accumulated a lifetime of general knowledge and stories to remember to pass my spare time.

Finally, we wish you all a Merry Christmas (if you are in America) or Gong Xi Fa Cai (if you are in China).

Henry & Peggy, 1988

Fiction

16

Comedy on the Whitecaps

by Henry Yu-Heng Ho
from his book *Comedy on the Whitecaps*, 1965

Photo: Original book cover of *Comedy on the Whitecaps*

My Dear Readers:

Before I begin this story, permit me to make two necessary or perhaps unnecessary declarations:
1. This is just a story. With flattery accepted, this is euphemistically known as creative writing. Therefore, please do not be overly suspicious in comparing this story with any known time, place, or people (including this storyteller) based on what you have heard or read elsewhere. Any similarities are purely coincidental.
2. This story illustrates some of the challenges in our profession as naval personnel. Since we have evacuated many of you to Taiwan ahead of the Communist occupation of China, we are ready to bring you back when our government [Nationalist] recovers China again. So part of this story may reoccur and prove useful to you (and me) in the future.

*****

This story occurs during history's darkest and most unfortunate hours when the red flame of communism consumed China like a wild forest fire. Our government decided that since the enemy could not be stopped, we would separate and extinguish this fire with water.

Therefore, all sea-going transport ships were drafted to ferry government and army personnel, educators, businesspeople, and many civilians across the seas. During this difficult time I, as a First Lieutenant on a navy transport, was but a small cog caught in this massive machinery. *(Translators' Note: Nearly one million soldiers and civilians were initially evacuated across the Taiwan Strait between 1949 and the early 1950s.)*

Perhaps you already know the duties of a Navigation Officer, a Communication Officer, a Weapons Officer, or an Engineering Officer on a naval ship. What, then, are the duties of a First Lieutenant? He picks up mostly hard-to-do and leftover jobs that others do not want. He organizes rust repairs and general clean-up activities, fixes the toilets and any leaks aboard ship, and more. . . . And yes, his duties even include dealing with passengers and cargo on board a transport.

At the time, those of us who served on navy transports envied, to the point of feeling sour grapes, those who were fighting on the front. We watched as others fought and earned medals or citations, all while being

Comedy on the Whitecaps

frequently catered to by civilian support groups. All we did was doggedly ferry people and goods across the Taiwan Strait from all parts of China. However, we took pride in performing our task while repeatedly sailing across the Strait. With the clock ticking and with each trip completed, more and more people and resources were being saved from enemy hands. While we understood the importance of our job in the overall picture, the intense, head-spinning schedule imposed from above often made us strangers to ourselves.

Often, we would receive a rushed message from fleet headquarters only miles after our departure from the China coast. It would read, "Upon arrival on xth day of xth month, discharge without delay and immediately return for next voyage."

Upon return to China and before the ship's gangway was lowered, crowds waiting on the pier would rush aboard as if it were a hundred-meter dash. From this moment on, the First Lieutenant became the most sought-after person to them. He also doubled as the ship's chief tea-serving steward. During the war, many who had passage for evacuation were often either high-ranking officials or those with special government connections. In any of the world's navies, the rank of the captain of a ship is no higher than Captain. However, the captain of our transport was only a Lieutenant Commander, a rank that is two levels below that of a full Captain. If you follow the hierarchy downward, I was two levels below him, thus had only one-and-a-half stripes on my sleeves. With so many big Buddhas descending upon our small floating temple, military etiquette would require that I stand at full attention at all times and never drop my saluting right hand. Indeed, these passengers had unique interests and individual requirements that could not be ignored by us.

"Are you the First Lieutenant? I am General Chen's chief of staff. The General and I even have the same surname." With a whooshing sound, Colonel Chen pulled out his huge calling card and shoved it right in front of my face. It had five or six official titles plus his rank and name in large print! Next, he handed me a long list of names. "Here is a list of names of the General, his full family, and staff members. This passenger list was approved by your Naval headquarters. Please arrange rooms for us."

Soon after Colonel Chen spoke, a nearby gentleman dressed in a well-tailored Western suit also pulled out his calling card. He spoke in an elegant voice but with an indignant "someone-has-ignored-me" red face. "Sorry," he said, "I am a commissioner from X Ministry's X Department.

I am charged with conveying these top-secret documents and valuable items. We need a separate room that is isolated from everyone."

"First Lieutenant, this officer has a letter of introduction from Admiral so-and-so." The ship's messenger brought another officer to me. "Please look at this calling card from Admiral Ding. Your Captain asked that you make arrangements for us."

During a busy moment, an unpleasant quarrel over how sidearms should be kept on board broke out. "A gun is a soldier's second life. How can I surrender it to you?" angrily declared the armed passenger to our gangway guard. He also had an "I'd rather die than give this up" expression.

I explained to him with a friendly face, "Friend, we do not want to take your second life, but your army and our navy regulations require us to hold your weapon for safe-keeping during the voyage."

"Then who is responsible for my security?"

"Hey . . ." I smiled at his large, attractive gun belt and holster while quickly assessing whether the owner was a cowboy-like shooter. I then resorted to my usual tricks to allay his anxiety. "We take care of the safety and security of all our passengers."

He still seemed hesitant, so I pulled him aside and asked in a low but caring tone, "Friend, have you ever been seasick?" At any sign of hesitation, I would have followed up with, "We expect foul weather ahead and with so many different characters on board, what if you become seasick and are unable to take care of yourself and lose the weapon? What will you say if you lose your gun?"

He gave quick thought to this and replied without losing his pride, "OK, I can let you hold on to my pistol. But I want an official receipt from your ship that includes the Captain's own chop."

"As you say, will do."

Before I could turn away, another passenger demanded, "May I ask what is the meaning of this? We have no place to lie down, and your officers' quarters are so spacious but off limits to us! I have traveled to many places in the world, but I have never seen any group so selfish. What kind of times are these? It is no time to snub us . . ." The man vented his anger and walked out without listening to our explanation.

Although there were numerous "diplomatic" incidents, there were plenty of domestic situations as well. The First Lieutenant became his shipmates' common target of ridicule. It seems that any passenger's misbehavior was the fault of the First Lieutenant.

Comedy on the Whitecaps

"Hey, we have passengers sleeping next to and on top of fuel valves. Are we going to sail or not?"

"First Lieutenant, sir. Someone is sleeping next to the main engine air inlets. If we turned on the fan, he would be sucked in."

"Attention, First Lieutenant!" came over the ship's PA system. "Please have your men advise the passengers not to sit in or sleep in the lifeboats."

"First Lieutenant, someone is urinating on deck. Is this not a naval vessel?"

After many such replays, our ship would finally be ready to sail. Things gradually returned to normal like a pool of muddy water that finally settles down in a clear lake. The First Lieutenant must next take care of the eating, drinking, toileting, and sleeping arrangements of his several hundred passengers.

Given sufficient time and space, all of this could be worked out. But, like the gentleman said, "What kind of troubled times are we in . . ." We were left to accommodate and be forgiving to each other on this overcrowded ship.

At the most inopportune moment, she appeared. I was tired, dirty, unable to focus, and cranky. At the time, I wished that I could just throw away my officer's hat and the job.

"Missus, I'll say it for you. You are the wife of an important official! You have an introduction letter! You have a calling card! You want a room! You want a bed! Fine, please find them yourself, anywhere you can."

"Will you please calm down?" she said in a composed but firm voice as she looked at me with her big and spirited eyes. She appeared neither angry nor fearful. I felt like I had been struck in the head by a club out of nowhere.

"If I were not traveling with these two children, I would not trouble you. I don't want a room or a bed. Neither will I mention who introduced me, nor who required a favor. We only ask that you assign us a place to shelter from the wind and the rain!"

Here was an amazingly tough lady, I thought to myself. How could I not help her? A missus traveling with two kids!

I brought her into the already crowded officers' quarters. I pointed at the space outside of my room (if you have been on a navy ship, you would know how small is the junior officers' room) and said, "Madam, please make do with this area. I am sorry, but I cannot give you my bed." It was a self-comforting line aimed at salvaging my pride. She did not thank me; I sensed that she thought poorly of me.

Our ship slowly steamed out of the harbor with the sun's remaining rays lazily setting behind us. The Officers Ward normally serves a light meal around 11:15 at night. It fills the stomach for those who are about to be relieved from their late evening watch and for those who were about to assume the next four-hour night watch. It also provides an occasion for us to socialize among our fellow officers.

Noodles were served on the first night. I was in my usual bad mood after a hectic day of loading the passengers. Knowing this, my shipmates started to tease me.

"First Lieutenant has a great job. Just look at how many people have to beg him . . ." said the Navigation Officer, who suffered from conjunctivitis, in an opening salvo in his Ningbo accent. I kept quiet.

"Of course," he continued, "those who are empowered get to do things their own way! What a prestigious job." Our Weapons Officer was my classmate and he knew how to needle me. Still, I kept quiet.

"First Lieutenant," said the Medical Officer, who was the least busy person on our ship, in his usual slow and soft voice, "I think if you can sell tickets, you can be a rich man."

I lifted my head above the noodle bowl, stared at each person, and replied in a fuming voice, "Gentlemen, if any of you wish to have this prestigious job or want to show off or get rich quick, you can have my job anytime. I will immediately request the Captain for re-assignment!"

The others had accomplished their goal of taunting me. They each had a smile but remained silent as they waited for me to continue. "Talk about a prestigious job," I said. Although by now I realized that I had fallen for their trick, I could not stop venting my frustrations. "Would you like to hear me recite some of the conversations I had today?" I then repeated the harsh remarks made earlier today by the "world traveler."

"Please tell me how this is prestigious? Although this ship is our home and workplace, I doubt even the Captain remembers what his room looks like? At least he has an alternative Captain's day room to rest. For you and me, we are officers who crowd out the petty officers. Petty officers crowd out the chiefs, while the chiefs crowd out the sailors. Everyone is under stress. Selfish, huh? I bet that after we dock, our passengers won't even remember what we have done, let alone thank us. They will simply disembark with pouted lips . . ."

At this time, I heard some bemused laughter that incited me to continue, "For example, you know that missus who is sleeping outside my room?" She said, 'Oh, please have some sympathy for me and my two kids, but I bet you that by tomorrow . . .'"

My audience gave a strange laugh, and some also coughed slightly. I got carried away and continued, "After she disembarks and if we should meet and sit together on the same bus, I guarantee that she will turn her head away and cover her nose." I covered my nose with my right hand and shook my head to mimic the point.

The Medical Officer stood up nodded toward the door and said, "Please come in . . ." My gosh, there she was. I got carried away and did not see her standing at the door of our Officers Ward. My face turned red all the way down to my neck.

"The children would like some water. Please have some sympathy for us," she said with an obvious sarcastic tone. I was too embarrassed to look at her. Some of my fellow officers burst into loud laughter as soon as she had gone.

On the second night, we had soup. The more sociable Weapons Officer brought us some news that further embarrassed me. "We should not call her a Mrs.! She is a Miss. Those two kids are her nephews. They are her brother's children, did all of you get that?" Although his explanation was for me, he was kind enough not to have mentioned my name.

"If you call a Mrs. a Miss, it is a compliment. But if you call a Miss a Mrs., it is considered bad manners. The way I see it, if she weren't trying to get a place on our ship, a slap in the face would have followed," said the Navigation Officer, who was a wise guy. This time I made sure that I sat facing the door.

The Medical Officer also chimed in, "Hmm . . . someone wants a girlfriend so much to get married, yet when a fish is biting he throws a rock in the water . . ."

I made up my mind not to be teased by them again. I also made up my mind to apologize to her. After dinner, I carefully walked past her as she was sitting on the floor. She was wrapped in a blanket while reading under the dimmed hallway lights.

"Miss . . ." I called lightly as she graciously lifted her head, "I am sorry that I called you by the wrong title, and . . ." I managed a sheepish smile.

"Is this why you are now polite to me?" She still had that calm, unafraid, and decisive look in her eyes. "You, sir, are a very good actor," she added as she looked me straight in the eyes.

I was bludgeoned by her yet again and even more this time. I did not know how I returned to my room. Lying in my bed, I wished I would not have to walk across that door again before she departed the ship. Better yet, I could ask someone to weld shut my door to its steel frame. I pulled at my hair and regretted my reckless behavior and foolish words. Suddenly, my bedside phone rang. It was the Captain ordering me to the bridge.

On the third evening, we had little appetite as the weather turned violent during the afternoon. Our ship sailed in front of a Mongolian cold front. The wind force greatly increased and so did our ship's motion due to heavy waves with whitecaps hitting us above deck. Those passengers who refused our seemingly nitpicking rules were now experiencing severe nausea. Unsecured luggage bounced around in the hold like uncontrolled air bubbles rolling in a level gauge. Those who berthed above deck were moved quickly inside. They were forced to leave behind their completely soaked luggage. The biting wind scattered blankets, cover sheets, and clothing all over the deck.

Except for a lucky few, all of the passengers were struck by seasickness. They lay down and were unable to take care of anything except themselves. Partially digested food mixed with green-yellowish stomach fluid became regurgitated as a nauseating mess. The passenger holds were full of acidic, foul, and raw odors. Such a scene made even us old deckhands swallow our saliva. Those who had never experienced rough seas were in terror. Some started to pray while women and children were crying.

Such a chaotic condition affected the ship's damage control precautions. The Captain ordered me to lead all available hands to secure the ship and to calm and comfort our passengers during this terrible storm.

To secure the ship meant to batten down all loose objects, which included removing all luggage obstructing our watertight doors. To calm meant to calm down all frightened passengers. To comfort meant slowing down the ship or changing course to lessen the waves' impact on the ship. After three to four hours of battling the storm and taking care of our passengers, things started to quiet down and become under control.

I thought about taking care of myself. I was dirty and my uniform was soaked with seawater and nauseating vomit. I needed to go back to my room to change and get ready for dinner. I walked back up to the Officers' Quarters, holding on to any hand railings I could find while being tossed left and right against the bulkheads. With much difficulty, I finally reached my room.

In front of my eyes and next to my door was a touching sight. My "under-the-eaves" guest, if I could call her that, was hugging both kids tightly with one arm while her other hand gripped tightly onto the rope-hooped handrail. Her face was the same color as a piece of plain paper held under a kerosene streetlight – frightfully blue. Her eyes were tightly shut. Her right hand was bruised from holding on to the rough rope surface of the handrail for a long time. Both kids were tired and half asleep; there were streaks of tears on their faces.

I dashed forward and moved to take both children from her. She opened her eyes slightly and then closed them again. She let go of the kids. I placed the youngsters in my bed. I took out the fastening belts underneath the mattress to buckle the kids to the bed. I then went out to help her. When she became aware that I was moving her into my room, she refused. "I am not going to your room," she said in her same decisive voice.

This time, I ignored her. I abruptly carried her in my arms and put her in my bed. I then said, "You can lie down here to watch the kids." I buckled her in with the kids. I wedged my trash can between the bed and the leg of my writing desk. "If you wish to throw up, use this. If the kids throw up, use the bed."

I opened my closet, took out a clean uniform, and hurriedly left my room. At the bridge, I reported the passengers' and ship's below decks status to the Captain. He listened while his eyes remained fixed on the huge waves striking the ship's bow as he gently massaged the leather strap of his binoculars as if he were counting rosary beads. After I finished my reporting, he gave a gentle smile and said, "Thank you for the hard work." That was my reward for the day.

In the chart room, I inquired about the ship's current position from the Navigation Officer. The ship's course had moved south to reduce discomfort to our passengers. I did a quick check of our current heading and said to the Navigation Officer, "Looks like we will be four hours behind schedule?"

He replied with humor, "What else can we do? We must treat our customers better for more business next time."

As I returned to my room, the ship's motions finally eased. After we passed Tai Chung City abeam, the Central Mountains of Taiwan shielded us from the northeasterly winds and the weather gradually improved. I remembered my hungry stomach so poured a half glass of water to wash down two dry biscuits.

The noise woke her. My guest turned around and greeted me. "It's 3:30 in the afternoon." She looked at her watch on her limp wrist.

"No, it's 3:30 in the morning," I replied with a smile.

She appeared surprised and asked me with a weak smile, "Oh, you never slept?"

"I just came off my watch." Thinking that she may not understand our maritime terminology, I added, "I meant I just finished driving the ship from the bridge."

As I tried to eat a biscuit, she suddenly retched. "Does food make you uncomfortable?" I put the biscuits back into their tin container and carefully covered its lid.

"I wonder how you can eat at a time like this?"

"To stay alive! Otherwise I will have to force myself to eat during a storm. If I didn't eat, I would have quit this job a long time ago."

"Is life at sea often like this?"

"Not always, but this storm is not that bad."

"Then what is a terrible storm like?"

"Oh." I thought about it quickly. "It's a bad storm when I lose my appetite." She laughed and this time showed a real smile. It was the first time we looked at each other with anything beyond rigid formality.

"Please go ahead with your eating. I am alright with it."

"Oh, it can wait. I'd prefer to talk with you for a while. We are now within sight of Taiwan and the weather has turned better."

"We could see Taiwan now?"

"Yes, but only from the radar. I can bring you topside later to have a closer look."

The sea now looked like a silky blue blanket suffused with soothing ripples. Fluffy white clouds intermittently covered the purple mountains in the distance. The shoreline could be seen covered with windbreaking trees with their leaves willowing like early spring buds. This entire scene was bathed under a gorgeous sun. This was Taiwan's welcome to her. After experiencing a night of a terrible storm, the island looked especially beautiful and friendly.

By now, most of the passengers had come up to enjoy the view. They were vying with each other to get a better view of their new home away from home. After a frightening night, the passengers got to know me better and were competing with each other to thank me for my help.

"You have now become everyone's hero," she complimented as she stood next to me. She also said philosophically, "When they see you in the future, I do not think they will turn their heads away or cover their noses." I felt embarrassed again.

As the ship prepared to enter port, I had to get these words off my chest. "I would like to apologize for calling you with the wrong salutation."

"Don't think much of it. Especially for us travelers, don't you think a 'Mrs.' salutation would be safer than a 'Miss' among strangers?" She again smiled calmly and continued, "However, being a Miss also has its advantages, no?"

When the voyage ended, her brother arrived from another town to pick her up. He thanked me for taking care of his sister and sons. When he heard that we were to leave the same night for Shanghai, he suggested, "Could we exchange addresses? We would be pleased to welcome your visit during shore leaves."

"I already have your address," I quickly replied.

When I received my next commission to become an Executive Officer of a frigate, my fellow officers gave me a send-off dinner. After some drinks and the usual pleasantries, they started to tease me again, but it did not work this time.

"Come on, you lucky person. Let us toast for your double fortunes so it may rub off on us." With this remark, the Weapons Officer emptied his glass of wine.

"Captain, sir," the Medical Officer still talked in his slow voice, "Weapons Officer would like to have the First Lieutenant post."

"Is that right?" The Captain joined the game and asked me, "I heard that you did not want this job when you first arrived?"

"Captain, sir, this is not true."

"Of course, you changed your mind after tasting its sweetness," the Navigation Officer said in a sarcastic tone. All broke out in laughter. I behaved like a groom pretending not to have heard a bad wedding toast, but inside I was absolutely delighted.

The Captain raised his glass and toasted, "First Lieutenant, thank you for your fine service aboard our ship. I wish you the best of luck, but the job of an Executive Officer is also very challenging."

"Thank you, Captain, for your teachings. Please forgive me for many jobs for which I did not perform as expected." I made sure to behave politely throughout the whole evening.

"You are a fine officer." The Captain raised his glass again. "My regards to your wife as she was also one of our passengers." Without saying thanks, I automatically raised and emptied my wine glass in one gulp.

"Indeed, when it comes to toasting his wife, he is so happy and drinks without being asked. Captain, sir, request that he be punished with another glass of wine."

"Let's take it easy on him." The Captain spoke softly like a brother. "With such a romantic precedent, I could see all of you will be fighting for the job of First Lieutenant when we return to China."

17

Typhoon Night

by Henry Yu-Heng Ho
from his book *Comedy on the Whitecaps*, 1965

Whenever he was lonely, he wished for a typhoon to descend upon the city, hoping for howling wind and torrential rain like Typhoon Dinah. During that storm's shocking display of nature's chaotic powers, his experience wasn't that of disaster and injury, but rather of an extraordinary dream that came to life. The dream's excitement, its heartwarming feelings, and an understanding of life with hypocrisy peeled away all occurred during that fearful night. As the wind died down and the clouds lifted, as the Earth once again returned to her bright and peaceful self, he once again resumed his "normal" lonely, monotonous, and hypocritical life. Yet that typhoon night left an unforgettable memory in his mind.

The weather changed as forecasted. Starting at noon the sky became lead black, there was an oddly uncomfortable feeling as if one's pores had been plugged. Occasionally, a cool and refreshing gust of wind brought a few raindrops, but not enough to wet clothes or dampen the street. Buses hung red signs saying "Typhoon Alert. Listen to Broadcasts." Like ships returning to port in a storm, the buses brought people home. Shop doors were half-opened. Offices also announced afternoon preventative measures, meaning there was no need to come to work.

He returned home, telling the driver to stop the car at the gate and go home. His coworker and roommate indeed went back to Hsinchu City to take care of his family. The Ah-po, their domestic helper, had prepared both his lunch and dinner, saying she would not be back in the afternoon. With the arrival of a disaster, it seemed everyone had a home to return to; everyone had their responsibilities and a place to take refuge. But his home was just this private house rented by his company. Other than his safety, there was nothing to worry about. He smiled with satisfaction, removing his clothes to begin his regular afternoon nap. During this unexpected "typhoon vacation," he could get some needed rest. He brought out a kung fu novel from under his pillow and lay down comfortably.

The wind was like a rogue beggar knocking again and again on unopened windows and doors, each time more violent than the next. After being woken, he couldn't fall asleep again. He felt for the book at the head of the bed, opened up a dog-eared page, and continued reading.

The contrast between the commotion outside and the excessively silent emptiness inside upset his usual "calm as still water" demeanor. He couldn't concentrate on his reading, so he might just as well toss away the book and get up. To pass the time in this interminable moment, he unnecessarily washed his face, slowly brushed his teeth, inspected every window and door, and looked at the dinner the Ah-Po had prepared in the kitchen. He sat down thinking about writing a letter to his wife Yaohua in the south. But after he took out a pen and paper, he hesitated about what to write. Love letters were too cliché. A letter home reporting all was well? It seemed it would be better to wait until after the typhoon had passed. Discuss the issue of moving the rest of their family to Taipei again? Actually, they'd discussed the pros and cons of coming or not coming for more than five years. Both parties' reasons were right. He raised his head to look at her picture on the table. She was pretty. The corners of her lips turned up in a smile on her oval face, which was covered by long, flowing hair, revealing a gentle yet resolute personality. The pair of glasses she wore made her even prettier, emphasizing her competence and intellect.

"I do love her, and she loves me," he thought. "It's just that the two of us both lack the power to make the other give up their current lifestyle so that we can live together like a normal married couple." He couldn't think of why and couldn't find who was at fault.

Typhoon Night

Outside, the sky grew even gloomier. The dropping air pressure irritated him. His slovenly bed reflected his state of mind. The emptiness of his colleague's bed across from him seemed only to mock him. He finally made up his mind to find some distraction outside and watch all the "commotion." As he drove his car out of the alley, he could already tell the strength of the wind had increased from the trembling of the canopy cover over his car. It rained harder. There weren't many pedestrians on the street. A few souls were huddled inside the bus stop waiting. Some hid beneath the pedestrian arcades to avoid the rain. People had to walk with bent waist into the wind with their heads turned away from the driving rain. Trishaw peddlers got off their seats and were pushing their carts hard against the wind. He chose a Cantonese restaurant and casually ordered something. By the time he finished his meal, the weather had worsened considerably. Raindrops swept in from the jeep's side canopy. Several stores' signs were rocking or swaying heavily in the wind. A police car drove by slowly. A female broadcaster's voice from inside the car shouted shrilly that the powerful typhoon's center would pass over the city at midnight and warned residents to take precautions against the wind and rain.

The sky darkened as if it were nighttime. He thought he shouldn't linger on the street any longer. In the few steps since he had taken since parking the car and going into the courtyard, the rain had already soaked his outer clothing. After witnessing the beginning of the chaos outside, his mood instead calmed. He changed into pajamas and prepared a flashlight, matches, and candles at his bedside. He brewed a new pot of tea and lay down, taking out the kung fu novel again.

He momentarily forgot about the storm outside his window and his earlier depressed mood. Perhaps because the so-called brave and chivalrous kung fu heroes and their tales were all far away from reality and their sword-fighting and martial arts techniques were ridiculously exaggerated, the reading was effortless. More importantly, it offered an escape from reality as the stories were neither emotive nor cerebral.

The phone rang. Its ringing sounded urgent on this stormy night. He picked up the receiver and asked, "Who is it?" The whistling wind and rain made it hard to hear. He tried hard to recall the caller when the name was given. Suddenly he remembered.

"Ah! Ruby! Where are you? What's up?"

"I was in Zong He County visiting a friend, but now I can't go back. Can you give me a ride?"

"Ruby, my driver already went home." He heard her disappointed hesitation and continued, "Where are you? I'll come get you."

He could hear the glee in her answer. "I'm outside of the police station over the bridge!"

He hung up the phone, quickly dressed, draped on his raincoat, and burst out the door. Once inside the car, he wiped the rain off his face. He started the engine and turned on the headlights. Their beams seemed to struggle to penetrate the dense drizzle. The windshield wipers rapidly swept away sheets of rain from the windshield, leaving only a small fan-shaped aperture for him to see the road ahead. Fortunately, there weren't many cars or people on the street. He counted only a few buses. He drove slowly while reminiscing.

"Ruby, that naughty child!" This was the stage line that he always associated with her.

"This is the seventh-grade little sister who is going to play the role of Ruby." The director brought her in and gently introduced her to the rest of the cast. "Come and meet your stage sister-in-law, older brother, Mrs. Wang, little boy, Mom, and your Dad." The director pointed at him.

Ruby nodded to each person, obediently greeting them. Only when she finally came to him, she bit her lower lip in a smile and shook her head. She rolled her big, dark eyes, innocent like a little fawn, meek and timid.

From then on, she lost her real name. Not only in the drama club, but everyone at school all called her Ruby. Everyone liked and pampered little Ruby.

That was the year he graduated and began life as a drifter. He quit college during his freshman year and joined the Youth Expeditionary Force that was sent to Burma. He lived in primitive jungles. He lived in strictly a man's world – marching, fighting and more. Life's changes were truly hard to fathom.

It rained harder and harder. As he drove along the riverbank, it was just like sailing a boat on the ocean. The wind pushed the pitiful little jeep backward. He shifted gears. The car's canopy trembled as if being twisted and torn by an invisible hand; rain poured down in torrents onto the windshield like a waterfall plunging off a cliff. The windshield wipers could not sweep away enough of an empty section to let him see ahead.

It was too dangerous. This wind might flip the jeep, with its high center of gravity, whenever it pleased. The rain already made him blind. How was he going to cross the bridge? He wanted to head back, but he thought about the little kid waiting for him in the storm.

Actually, Ruby wasn't a young child anymore. She had experienced the same significant changes in life as he had. But after ten years, she still hadn't lost her former innocence and mischievousness. That pair of Bambi-like eyes hadn't changed.

He drove the car alongside a building so it could block the howling wind. He stopped and quickly ripped out both canvas side doors from the jeep. Although this would allow the wind to blow through either side, he could stick his head out into the rain to get a better view of the road ahead.

His jeep dashed onto the bridge. It truly seemed like the wind would lift the car, so he didn't know when he would be blown into the river below. The raindrops struck hard and hurt his face. He repeatedly blinked hard to rid the water pouring down his forehead and eyebrows. He seemed to be the only one on the entire bridge and maybe the only person outdoors in the entire city. He stopped his mindless speculating and instead focused on getting the car to his destination, thinking it was just like fighting through the monsoon season in Burma. Perhaps that special soldier's sense of "get-the-job-done" was still in him.

In the distance, he saw the red light of the police station. He sped up and honked the horn. The fuzzy shadow of a person appeared within the white beam of his headlights.

"Ruby!" he yelled, stopping the car.

She stepped into the car like someone crawling ashore.

"I knew you'd come," she shouted joyfully.

"I almost didn't make it!" He focused on turning his head back and reversing the car to turn around. Rain sprayed in from Ruby's side. She shifted toward him.

"I was thinking I shouldn't have called you."

"It's too late for that." His head was still stretched outside of the car.

The car went over the bridge again. Although the wind was just as fierce, with another person inside he felt relieved. Another gust of wind hit. Ruby made a sharp squealing sound and hurriedly grabbed his arm.

"Do you know how to pray?" he called.

"Yes!"

"Okay. You pray, I'll drive. Maybe the car can make it over the bridge."

He gripped the steering wheel tightly while searching ahead with his eyes and using the bridge's side posts to guide his steering. They appeared one and after another though barely reflecting his headlights in the blackness of the storm. He held his breath yet he could still taste the sweet raindrops through his opened mouth.

It wasn't easy to cross the bridge. The car finally coasted off the end of the bridge and onto a street where houses and buildings on both sides provided some relief from the wind. This was much better than being on the bridge. He pulled his head back inside the car. Ruby realizing that she was cuddled up close to him, quickly blurted in a self-mocking manner, "You're soaking wet!"

"Speak for yourself."

Ruby laughed. "I didn't even notice. I was really scared when we crossed the bridge just now."

"Did you pray for us?"

"More than prayed, I was crying loudly inside for help."

The low-lying areas of the city had already flooded. The water stirred up by passing cars hit the jeep's chassis and fenders in wave after wave, shaking its passengers each time. Pelted by rain the size of beans, the entire car seemed to be wrapped in water. As they crossed an alley, wind from the sides acted like robbers hidden in the shadows who strike without warning. The streets were already littered with broken branches, bamboo mats, and metal siding from shanties. The car approached the downtown area again but instead turned away toward the Xindian District. For this tiny and stubborn jeep, the rage of a typhoon was inexplicable, like an evil brigand shaking down a clueless and good citizen, swooping down on them over and over again. The car could no longer maintain a straight line through the chaotic streets. As he downshifted into second gear, Ruby threw herself into him, using a handkerchief to wipe the rain off his face.

"This is too dangerous," he called with his head still craned outside the jeep. "The wind outside the city must be even worse. Trees might be blocking the road."

"Then what shall we do?" Ruby was anxious.

"Ride out the storm at my place for a while."

"Alright, quickly then!" Ruby's heart was filled with fear. At the same time, she felt responsible and was more apologetic for being the cause of all the dangers and consequences that night.

Once the car turned to follow the wind, the situation was much improved. He could bring his head back inside. The typhoon had the entire city at her feet. People stayed inside their homes with the windows and doors tightly shut. The dim, yellow streetlamps were the only witnesses to this abusive insult to the city. Who knew how long these weak lights could keep watch to the spectacle?

"I feel so bad!" Ruby whispered in his ear.

"Ah, it was my decision." He smiled, still focused on driving. Water from his hair continuously flowed down onto his face. Ruby helped him wipe the water away with her hand. Seeing his own alley ahead, he relaxed.

He parked the car. In the dark, he fumbled to put back the side doors. At this point, as if appreciating a cherished horse, he patted the hood of the car and murmured, "You were a great help." He then held Ruby's hand and led her into the house.

He removed his raingear, but his clothes underneath were even wetter. The water in his shoes squelched as he walked. Like a naughty child who had just returned from playing with water outside, Ruby happily shook the water from her hair. He raised his gaze and had a good look at her for the first time this evening. Her looks stunned him.

Her usual fluffy, curly hair was now almost completely straight, stuck to her head. Her black yet shiny hair seemed to be covered with a thin layer of grease. She wore a close-fitting qipao with a duck eggshell-like bluish-green color decorated with red safflower embroidery that was practically part of her body. It tightly wrapped her ripe, luscious, and well-proportioned body, almost to the point of bursting. The open collar and slit revealed her neck and calf. Perhaps it was being bathed in rainwater, or perhaps it was the cold that made her pearly, supple skin seem fairer.

"What's wrong? Are you considering whether or not to let me in?" Ruby asked with a laugh.

"Oh, seeing you like this, I didn't recognize you. How could you go out without a raincoat?"

"I planned on going home early. Unfortunately, the married couple hosting me quarreled. I had to stay behind and play peacekeeper."

"Come on. Use the shower while I find some clothes for you to change into. My roommate Lao Wang went to Hsinchu, so there won't be anyone in the house." He didn't know why he added that last part. He opened his wardrobe closet, hesitantly rummaging through it for a pair of pajamas and a towel.

"Ruby. This is a 'beach outfit' given to me by a friend when he came back from America. Although it is a bit garish, it might fit. And here's a towel."

Shutting the bathroom door, he wiped himself dry in the kitchen and changed into dry underwear and pajamas. In the living room he brewed a cup of tea, lit a cigarette, and sat down.

Ruby had become a busy young woman. He occasionally heard his friends talking about her. He didn't see her again until she ended her unsatisfactory marriage and resumed her career. They had seen each other intermittently, and she also visited him but always when accompanied by other old friends. Then he would always act like a retired actor sitting offstage watching Ruby playing different roles onstage. He had also heard both compliments and criticisms of Ruby. Yet, she remained in his heart as the same actress he had first met. As time passed, she was able to act more and more.

"Did you just change costume again?" He regarded Ruby, who was standing at the entrance to the living room, as he leaned against the back of the couch motionless while amusedly enjoying the view.

Ruby seemed to guess his mood. She spread out her hands. The sleeves hung down and covered her hands while she spun around.

Women who wear men's clothing . . . although they seem amusing and cute, there's another kind of charm to them, he thought.

"I hung my wet clothes in your bedroom. The fan should dry them a little faster. Is that okay?" Ruby asked, tilting her head.

"This house doesn't have a host. Make yourself at home," he offered and gestured to the couch.

"You mean a lady of the house?" Ruby laughed as she sat down.

"I'm saying even I'm a guest here."

In the silence, they could again hear the howling wind outside, followed by the shaking of windows, doors, and even the whole house under tremendous air pressure.

"It's really windy!" he said.

"I'm really out of luck today, running into this big mess."

"Playing peacekeeper doesn't help you accumulate good karma!" he said.

"I take no credit for it. When life and property are threatened in this kind of weather, what is there to fight about? After seeing a young married couple in such a difficult situation, I just had to leave."

"Why did you think to call me?" He had been wanting to ask for a while.

"Because you have a car!" Ruby replied quickly without thinking too deeply. She purposefully followed with a witty retort, "Why did you come?"

"Mmm . . ." He held his cup with both hands, sipping a mouthful of tea. "Didn't I play your father?"

"You are most annoying!" Ruby glanced sideways at him. The mood in the room seemed to go back to over a decade ago when they were both students, just as intimate and carefree.

"Time has passed so quickly. We've changed a lot." He couldn't help but sigh.

"Tell me about it! Look at me." Ruby forced a smile.

"Do you think it's better to be married or to be like you are now?"

"Of course girls want to get married. But it can't be about fighting like the couple I went to see today," Ruby said, her voice still tinged with emotion.

"Some people say quarreling balances the state of mind in the life of a married couple."

"Nonsense!" Ruby looked at the photo on the table. "Do you and your wife fight?"

"No, not once." He thought of the horrible calm and rational relationship between them as husband and wife. They treated each other like guests.

"Of course, you two must be happy," Ruby praised.

"Are we?" he replied.

"Aren't you?" she retorted.

He was rendered speechless by her reply and nodded. He thought about Yaohua's aggressive career ambition and her calm consideration of the pros and cons of matters. She was always right. Yet, underneath that male psyche of his, there lived an impulse to have an all-out argument with her and then madly tell her how much he loved her and that he couldn't live without her.

Ruby sensed his ambivalence but couldn't guess at what exactly the problem between him and his wife was or how deep it had become.

Slowly she said, "It's hard to speak of the emotions between people. When I broke up with him, most people couldn't understand. His money and status were reasons to make most girls envious. But I threw that away."

"Why?"

"In this troubled world and with an inner desire to seek security, girls are of course a little more realistic. It's hard to speak of love on an empty stomach. But this has its limits. A house and a car aren't necessarily what every girl wants, while marrying just for love also sounds a bit corny. There must exist some kind of force that can bind two willing people to spend their lives together."

Suddenly, he discovered Ruby wasn't a child anymore. She had become a sensible and even thoroughly reasonable woman. He stared at her in surprise and asked, "Then you didn't have any love between you, or was it the notion of being willing to live your lives together?"

"No," she spoke again. "I wouldn't say that. He treated me very well, and this naturally included satisfying material needs. He also understood there was no love between us, even if it is the feeling a married couple should have. His loving me was a way to satisfy his possessive desire, seeped with his apprehensions of reputation and face-saving. He even tried his best to redeem this tragedy, but I'd made up my mind. In the end," she smiled a little, "he yielded. In people's opinion, I won all of the sympathy, while he took the censure."

"You don't seem like a heartless person." Based on the pair of small, white bare feet Ruby had, she should be a typical delicate, timid, and kind-hearted young lady.

"Heartless? How can you call me that? You don't know him. Speaking of him, he was still someone I should call "Uncle" since he was my father's friend. When I left my hometown to attend college in Nanjing, my father asked him to look after me. It's just that . . . for a girl like me, who should have been almost like a niece to him, he was too attentive." Ruby smiled bitterly. "But you can only blame it on my being too young. I really was a child back then." She pouted her lips slightly while blinking that pair of fawn-like eyes again. She stopped, then continued to speak.

"After I lost my innocence to him . . . I was horrified, ashamed, disappointed, bitterly filled with regret. I was forced to bow my head to him."

"You never had any children?"

"It's hard to believe. After we were finally married, we were husband and wife in name only. At night, I did not yield to his coaxing and pleadings nor did I succumb to the physical abuses brought on by his grudge against me. I did not stop him from finding another woman and even wished that he would. The past several years have been a torment. All I wanted from him was my freedom."

Her eyes teared up as her sorrow stirred sympathy in him. He was at a loss. He was listening to a story that he already knew the outcome of before the ending was revealed. The main character and storyteller was sitting right before his eyes. Was it a tragedy? Was it a farce? Was it right? Was it wrong? There was no good answer. Yet Ruby's honest and intimate revelations of her private affairs reminded him of the fantasies he'd occasionally have about her all those years ago. "If she married me . . ." Naturally, he was the same as any other man who often had those sorts of fantasies.

During this pause, he didn't hear the pressing storm outside the window. He put on and maintained a gentle smile typical of a caring elder. In his mind he imagined an empty bedroom at midnight where a man from an older generation was tempting, pleading, insulting, and beating a young girl. The man's face was ridiculous, despicable, and fiercely hideous. But in the dark of night and in other corners of the world, who knew how many similar performances there had been? It was rare to find a young woman with such indomitable determination and will.

Seeing his distracted expression, Ruby smiled gently.

"What? You don't believe me?"

"It's not that. You're truly a great woman."

"What's so great about this? Especially for Chinese women, divorce is a scar. What's more, I left in such a pitiful state. Other than the clothes on my back, I didn't have $100 [New Taiwan dollars] to my name. This was less than what he tipped his subordinates, but that was what I earned as a substitute teacher for a friend." She proudly continued, "The bitter days that followed are difficult to talk about. At first, I even walked to save on bus fare."

Moved, he stroked the back of Ruby's hand resting on the coffee table. She didn't shy away and responded with a grateful and graceful smile. He withdrew his abruptly placed hand with embarrassment and felt uneasy.

The lights dimmed, then brightened. The house seemed to be a pressurized tea kettle, and he didn't know when it would exceed its critical breaking point. The rain sounded like scattering beans, crisply hitting the windows and roof. The wind and rain separated the two of them from the outside world. He and Ruby – a young woman wearing baggy men's pajamas, a beautiful and seductive woman. His heart skipped a beat and suddenly raced, prompting a strange urge. The lights suddenly dimmed again, as if trying to provoke him, then stopped everything. He gently squeezed Ruby's hand, then released it and stood up.

"I will go and prepare some candles. You never know when the power will go out."

Walking out from the living room, he took a deep breath, trying to calm himself down. As he walked into the bedroom, Ruby's half-dried qipao dress swayed in the breeze from the electric fan. As if to escape, he grabbed the candle and hastily left the bedroom.

He didn't dare let his gaze linger on Ruby, who kept smiling at him.

"Why don't you remarry?" His question also seemed out of character for him.

"Who said I won't remarry again?" she replied good-naturedly. "Marriage is part of a normal life for men and women. But for a woman with pain from divorce, she has already lost a girl's impulsiveness for a first love so she needs to be much more careful. No one wants a second divorce. She would have to accept both the good and the bad and be calm and objective about it."

"And what are your thoughts?"

"Oh," she exhaled, tilting her head to think. "I am an ordinary woman. I love my home, decorated the way I like it. I don't hate the kitchen; cooking is a kind of joy. I like children – that should be an inherent nature for us women. As for men, they have to . . ." She bit her lip gingerly. "To speak bluntly, they have to convince me it's worth it for me to love them."

"That's truly a scale without standards," he laughed.

She paused, only to raise her eyebrows.

"Maybe I'm unlucky," she joked. It seemed she had returned to the innocent and mischievous little girl from those years ago, but in the blink of an eye, Ruby was still the mature Ruby. She continued, "Although I now have a good job and salary, there are some sincere and insincere men who orbit me like satellites. My life is free. No normal woman wouldn't want to have a family. But since I have difficulty with the tradeoffs involved, it is better for me to wait and see."

Just as he was about to say, "I wish you the best," a nearby tree trunk nearby was snapped by the wind. Its loud crack mixed with the howling wind and heavy rain were alarming enough to push one's heart to race. Soon after, the lights went out.

He hastened to light the candles. As the candle wick gradually turned into a bright but flickering light, Ruby's flirtatious look became even more alluring. Her ample breasts peeking through the open collar of her pajamas were drawing him like an irresistible magnetic force. All this made him rather uncomfortable.

"You should rest. You must be tired." He restrained himself.

She stood up after him. "You should be the tired one. I don't know why I'm babbling tonight . . ." She turned her head to the side and paused for a moment.

"Maybe it's to thank you for risking yourself in coming to pick me up. Maybe it's trying to apologize. Or maybe . . ."

"Maybe it's the typhoon," he said. "Come, I'll lead." He smiled, picking up the candle with one hand while extending the other to hold her hand. Unable to control himself, his hand trembled slightly.

"You've caught a cold!" Ruby said as she grasped his hand. He knew this was Ruby's excuse to change the subject and masked his action.

"No I haven't." Suddenly he turned and drew her toward him. Ruby didn't resist. He quickly recalled a scene from *War and Peace:*

> Pierre once said to Natasha: "If I were free, I would be on my knees this minute to beg for your hand and your love."

Involuntarily, he held her face, whispering the line in her ear. Ruby didn't speak. Her eyes fluttered slightly closed, and she looked at him with a smile of understanding, friendship, and empathy.

A drop of wax dripped onto his hand. Right, he wasn't free. He also wouldn't repeat that ugly performance that Ruby had just described. He couldn't, on this stormy night, carve another scar into this girl.

He settled Ruby on his bed and lit another candle from the bedside table. He took the kung fu novel from under the pillow and turned around to leave the bedroom.

"You don't want to sleep here?" Ruby hinted at the bed across from her.

"I want to read for a bit."

"Thank you." These seemed to be her final words for the night.

His heart calmed down much more. He sank deeply into the couch, used his foot to pull over a chair to prop his leg, and lit a cigarette.

Family, children, tasty homecooked dishes . . . that was the ordinary life people yearned for.

Outside, the gale abruptly died as the eye of the typhoon passed through. It was so calm you could even hear people turning in their beds. The living room seemed even more bleak and bare. They were only two candles that had stopped flickering, each now holding on to a heart at peace.

Remembrances

18

Henry Ho

October 23, 1990

Henry Yu-Heng Ho, also known by his pen name 雨痕 (Raindrop Streaks), was born on January 15, 1925. He was the youngest of two children from a tenant farmer's family in Liu Yang (瀏陽) city of Hunan Province (湖南), China.

In 1944, he left Chongqing University after only one month of study to answer the nation's call for the educated youth to fight against the Japanese Invasion. This movement was also known as the One Hundred Thousand Youth Join to Fight (十萬青年十萬軍).

He entered the Army Logistic College and in 1945 was assigned to the Nationalist Navy's Ships Take-Over Program (英国接艦) in England. He was trained as a weaponry repair specialist at the Royal Navy's Gunnery School at Whale Island, U.K. before being assigned to the light cruiser SS Chongqing (formerly HMS Aurora) in 1948. In the early 1950s, he graduated from the Naval Academy in Zouying (左營), Taiwan and continued to serve in the Navy for over twenty years. During his naval career, he completed both shore and sea duties. These included two tours as ship's Captain and serving as Assistant to the Chief of Navy. During his military career he received six naval service merit medals.

Upon his retirement from the Navy in early 1966, he worked in merchant marine industry at firms including Island Navigation, Oriental Overseas Lines, World-Wide Shipping, and Center Point Marine in a number of roles including Captain, Port Captain, and also Senior Operations Manager.

Henry married Peggy Hsueh in 1949 in Taiwan. They raised two sons, David and Peter. In 1966 the family immigrated to the United States. At the time, he wrote, "It is my great hope that my sons will be brought up and educated in this country for a better life and to be useful to society and mankind." David graduated from Columbia University, while Peter graduated from Johns Hopkins University before completing his M.D./Ph.D. studies at Yale University.

Throughout his life, Henry enjoyed his two favorite hobbies: writing and home do-it-yourself maintenance and repair.

Henry was an editor for his middle school newspaper and poster bulletins. He had a lifelong love of writing. After training in England, where he improved his English language fluency, he became interested in translating English works ranging from fictional and non-fictional literature to biographies to naval instruction manuals for Chinese readers in Taiwan.

He published two original books of short stories: *Blue Water Memories* and *Comedy on the Whitecaps*. He translated thirteen books from English to Chinese. He also contributed regularly to news and travel magazines published in Hong Kong as well as naval magazines and newspapers published in Taiwan. Driven by his passion to write, he often worked late into the night before resuming his regular work the next morning. He could write anywhere – in a hotel, on a train, or in an airplane – an impressive feat during the days before portable typewriters or computer word processors. After migrating to the States, he often published pieces (some co-authored with wife Peggy) about his travels and observations of the U.S. and other countries as a way to share the outside world with readers in Asia.

When he was not writing, he took delight in learning and then putting into practice these home DIY repairs, not only for our own home but at the homes of any friend who needed it. This resulted in weekly, sometimes even daily, trips to hardware and home improvement stores such as Rickles and Home Depot. He often spent hours browsing their aisles and asking store specialists questions about how to install or repair items in the home. He quickly became the most dependable resource for friends having house problems; he was more reliable than the plumber or electrician. He would often be found with sleeves rolled up and toolbox in hand, at any and all hours, in countless basements, bathrooms, and rooftops around northern New Jersey. He always dreamed of building his own house and finally was able to do so in 1988 in Fort Lee, NJ, the last home he would own.

Photo: Henry and Peggy Ho with David and Peter in Taiwan, 1964

19

Peggy Ho

May 13, 2010

It is always challenging to summarize a life in a few minutes, especially a life of eighty-two years as full as my mother's. But when I think of her, three words come to mind – toughness, determination, and sacrifice.

I

First and foremost, David and I and our children know our mother to be tough. Tough not in that she was mean-spirited, but tough in that she had endured many difficulties in her life and overcome many obstacles to achieve all that she did. Mom lived through the wars in China during the 1930s and 1940s. She told us of days of eating rice flavored only with lard and mixed with stones so that there seemed to be more food than there was. She told us of sheltering in caves during air bombings and having to move to different cities to get away from the fighting. Some of you may know that Mom did not like cats. You may not know the reason is because she had to step over so many dead cats in the streets while walking to school during wartime.

But Mom's biggest battle was not World War II, but her long battle with cancer, which she had won for nearly twenty-five years. In 1985, she developed breast cancer. I can still remember the utter despair on my father's face when they first heard from the doctor. But Mom bore down and put herself through what needed to be done. She had surgery and then started chemotherapy. I will never forget the days that she would come home after receiving chemotherapy. The drugs were terrible for making her terribly nauseous. At home, I would find her lying down, many times right on the kitchen floor, lying very still trying not to vomit as the waves of nausea washed over her. Yet despite this, she would drive herself to the hospital fifty miles there and fifty miles back each time even though she knew the treatment would make her very sick. And as a result, she beat the odds and her breast cancer never came back. I think her cancer was probably a little afraid of her.

But Mom did develop a second cancer – nasopharyngeal carcinoma – three years ago. She knew she was in for a rough time. The treatment of radiation and chemotherapy was even harder than for her breast cancer. Besides, she was seventy-nine years old, not in her fifties. But she survived once again and resumed her independent life living in Fort Lee. Mom was deeply religious and she greatly enjoyed attending church services and Bible study and spending time with her dear friends here. Ultimately, she would not win this battle, and her cancer came back this August. She responded to the devastating news with the dignity and grace that we have come to expect of her. After hearing the medical options, which were not good, she thought about it and told us, "I want to go naturally."

Mom's toughness was not lost among her grandchildren. She played a big role in raising David's daughters, Clara and Candace, who got to know her well when they were children and teenagers. There are two quotes from them about their Popo that I will always remember. Clara always remarked, "Popo is really strong." Candace has frequently said, "Popo can do anything, after all, she's Peggy Ho."

However, even when times were tough on her, Mom always went out of her way to be kind to others and acknowledge their help. When I brought her back from Hong Kong to the U.S. in August after her cancer had come back, she was weak so we arranged at each of the airports — Hong Kong, Tokyo, and Newark — to have a wheelchair for her. The airlines always sent someone to wheel her through the terminal. Even though she had just been told she had terminal cancer, she insisted upon giving a tip to the aides who pushed her wheelchair. I had not thought ahead and prepared for this. I did not have any Hong Kong dollars or Japanese yen, so she insisted that we still give them a tip with U.S.

currency to recognize their assistance. Similarly, as the end neared our local hospice arranged to have a person come to our home three times a week to give Mom a bath. After her first bath from Yuki, Mom discreetly turned to me and said, "Give me $20." This as she was facing her impending death.

II

The second word that comes to mind is determination. When Mom was a child, she was sent to live with her aunt in Shanghai. I think it always hurt her that she did not grow up in the same household as the rest of her family during her younger years. She was not encouraged to further her education beyond secondary school. But she studied hard and on her own found a way to go to nursing school and become a professional. Later in life, she would be one of the first nurses to become qualified to work in the cardiac intensive care units, which were then just being established in hospitals. I remember the thick textbooks that she would bring home and study at night while I was doing my homework from elementary school.

Mom married my father over the initial objections of her parents, and he ultimately proved to be the good husband and worthy son-in-law that Mom saw in him. Leaving all that they had behind, she and my father left China to start a new life in Taiwan. Later, when they saw opportunities for a better life for David and me in the U.S., they once again left behind a very comfortable life in Taiwan and risked becoming strangers in a strange land. Today, I am not sure I would have had the courage and drive to make those same decisions and put my own life and my family's in that much upheaval. But it was a great decision and one that our family appreciates greatly. This also goes to show that when Mom wants something, she gets it over any and all obstacles.

III

The third operative word for Mom is "sacrifice." And there is no question that she sacrificed much of herself for all of us. I just told you about their transitions from China to Taiwan to the U.S. Another example is in the work that she chose. For most of Mom's years as a nurse, she worked the overnight shift, 11 p.m. to 7 a.m. She did it because the pay was better so she could better provide for us. It also meant that she kept very different hours than the rest of the family. When I would come home from grade school, Mom would be asleep. Later, she would wake up to prepare dinner and spend the evening hours with us, helping me with my homework, before leaving the house to go back to work just as the rest of us were going to bed. One of my dearest memories is from when I was in first and second grade. I would walk home for lunch, open the front door with the key attached to the chain around my neck, and find a TV dinner in the oven waiting for me. Mom always put a TV dinner to cook before she went to sleep in the mornings so there would be something hot for me to eat. And I knew that even though I didn't see her much, she was thinking about me and watching out for me.

In the end, Mom's illness served to bring us, her children and grandchildren, together. We are spread out geographically – David and Lisa in Hong Kong, Clara in Chicago, Candace in New York, and my family in Delaware. It is too easy to get wrapped up in our own lives and careers and forget about one another. We would all be together once, at most twice, a year. But since Mom's cancer relapse, we have spent more time together than at any time in the past. We've had to think together and work together in helping to make Mom comfortable in her remaining time as she slowly lost her abilities. And in doing so, we helped each other in ways that we did not have to do when separated and leading our own lives. And that is something that we are all thankful for.

I'd like to close with a little story about one memory that always springs to mind first when I think of Mom. I was eight years old and wanted to go to a store with my friends to buy something. I asked Mom, trying to convince her with the argument that "all my friends are doing this," and she said no. The next day I asked her again and she said no. The third day I tried again and got the same answer. Finally, on the fifth day, she looked down at me and said, "I'm your mother. I don't negotiate." I learned very quickly that Mom is tough; she is more determined than I was; and, while she will sacrifice anything for me, she won't sacrifice her principles when she is right.

Mom, thank you for loving us, teaching us, and raising us. You are in our memories forever.

Photo: Peggy and Peter Ho in Taiwan, 1963

Original Chinese Articles

A Sampling

Game of Checkers in Life

生命的棋局

珮琪

但願人長久　千里共嬋娟

裡，一個過碼頭官，九年以前，他是海軍陸戰隊員，九年以前，他是海軍穿的制服。

然而我是嫁給了他，轉眼已屆九年，這九年之中，嘗盡多變的世味，豈嘴唸到了五味的人生。這個美滿的姻緣，證明了我九年換作的正確。如我跪在鈑了九個海外，覺得起書本在課讀，但往事歷歷在目，心頭益多慮的病者的良旺同事，而且塵上一毛病——鼻蝶炎。

民國三十七年，在我服務的病房裡，有混進一對人：他們都是剛從國外接收軍艦上的同事，而新從國外接收軍艦上的同事，而手術完成後的星期天下午，我孤零零地人體睡眠的呼吸，十一點的小夜班任何一個，還且他們多了一條開過了力，結果良好，這是第二次出現在辦公室的門口。

「第九床？」我想不起這個人和他所指跟著床是怎麼回事。

「小姐，隔壁病床病有入氣皿了。」一個圓孔顯得叫衡的人和出現在辦公室的門口。

「我到底是怎麼一回事？」我像神話因嘴唇不能勤揮而顯得困難。他脫說話因嘴唇不能勤揮而顯得困難。

治大夫並沒有留下什麼特別的O關照護應，手術進行良好，主流到口腔，速成帶粘液從口鼻出。病人是暢口出血，從內鼻孔der。不用說我，就是值班的醫生都嚇得面無人色。普通的辦法對我除了應急止血外，對此特殊的方法，加上星期六找不到人是感了的，情形不是容易的，再加上舟車勞頓的，一個對於出血的情形，他不像一般病人，或是親友哭的事，也不像一般病人，或是親友哭的事。這個同病相憐的人對他的悲苦他也並不深記，他的指身意悲苦他也並不深話他什麼，或是夏光內行似的拍打，他只是靜靜躺在病床上休息，當他發生粗重的流血勞動過度，也發生粗重的呼吸，他搖頭從嚼動中叶出一句：

「我們是一對呀！」

小夜班在工作上是輕鬆一些，每日黃昏除了休息之外，第九床竟在我的工作場合中，自從那個星期後的第九床，都不敢輕易離開。他從後得很小心，且是第十床他接到敷對他很可酸慢，且是第十床他很有禮貌，雖一切如常了。他常常在經過辦公室的當兒，有時沒事進來聊聊天，我不能說他是受歡迎的，但也並不討厭。

有一回似乎話說盡了，他順手拿起桌上角上的跳棋，打開看看問道：「小姐這是跳棋嗎？」

「是的，你會下嗎？」我那時是剛學會不久，與幾挺深的。

「他退了是，才帶笑地說：」

「那麼我教你。」

我問他說明下棋的沒法，一直也不說出去，攔開了棋盤然的一點下棋後自己給了他一些，但他比我更容易，因為沒有下過跳，反而帶了便從以前，有時分分明明，跳過了陣橋的棋子，但他一步不以勝利者，便從心理觀念，也有時勸讓我好勉從事我已懵懵面嘆過幾步，他總會有棋子在孤單單地掉在後面。

面對一個初學的人，本不能多怪，我是很有信心了，便多找出過，不過這便太慢，又好像我在跳棋似的，可以無便高興有這麼的快感，來去他的步子。一個一個幾棋時的愉快，與第九床無事時的正比的，有一天我們約下跳棋，我正在淺著一些圍棋書找我盤在下棋時太深入，飛過公事來來到辦公室，立刻的身後，

他說：「小姐，跟我他退著忙用手塊從的名手。」

這是我們缺棋名手。

我晴著，更捂飾的多時蘊起身後的多手打她，更捂飾的多

鴛鴦蝶之情

徵文第三名

「別講騖話，我的棋還是剛從小姐這裡學會的。」

當然我并不是下了那盤棋就訂後面的同伴自然會意，我也把一切都看在眼裡，認爲他不應該裝儍作乎人，我是受了欺騙。

可是一件事從不同角度去衡量，會產生不同的結論；下班後我獨自坐在桌上，同味這件事又有必要，木來下棋是件娛樂，他眞？或者他是爲了討我的歡欣之一。故意地把他的棋下得高，讓我特意地走那些不高明的踏腳石，他是爲了做我的踏腳石，之，他也許是個體貼入微的人，他可能有一個溫柔的個性，還是促成我日後嫁給他的理由之一。

我娶棋，或者是爲了討我的歡欣倒是。是爲了訪問我的賭懷？我們的婚姻生活，很像這局棋的複雜。當然我們有意見不一時，不爭執們到海軍碼頭迎着小火輪戰出的黃浦江口而去，心中五味俱陳。局勢雖在人羣中高唱靑春舞曲，他是那樣地快樂地送他回醫院去療養一般，凱旋歸化裝舞會，我們在四川路的凱旋飯店裡晚餐。那晚，我們在第一一下，上海是有些風聲鶴唳。但我千里迢迢地再回到這沿海的大城來，鄉下看母親了，世局幻變又將息的家一切都看在眼裡，認爲他不應該裝傻作乎人，我是受了欺騙。

他從船上帶來的 Dry Gin。夜深了，我有怪，自己也不會怎麼水手的氣息。

開春後他的艦修好了，又再出海作戰。在一個海霧的清晨，我途經着化裝的埃及式水桶帽，一手挽着沒有上次那樣的惨怕，台灣是復興的基地。同時，我已立即答應嫁他的草人形和焦點。人心動盪，前路迷惘，他匆匆地接到上海去台灣。這次，我再在江邊途別他的時候，這八年的日子只是只有抒於佳境的感。目前，這是最壞的情況了。那反面因爲他的誠實，而我反覺得女朋友歡心的必要手段了，但我獲得什麼空白的允諾，或者僞師的吹噓，我有怪，自己也不會怎麼頭腦了一顆仁慈的心，始終他不曾給過什麼東西了，不過我在想，一套服外也再沒有東西了，不過我在想，一套服外也再沒有他的財物，可以帶他一個聰明的叛變對海軍的影響，他痛哭得像一個孩子。

船上工作，不過，我一想到這條軍艦叛變對海軍的影響，他痛哭得像一個孩子。他喜歡旅行，他就在跟着我一個牧童。他自然有天下了。他曾坦白的說愛他，他聯想到它，可能給我和災難中的蓄逃，聯想到它，可能給我和災中打過，我在家中打過海軍太太的小坎上，知道在這個時候，她們的「人」，不知道會來迎接他們歸來。

在這個戰爭中船開到什麼地方去，作什麼，好久會囘來？那是無法知曉的。自然日子長了也慣之了。

四十三年，正趕上人們準備新衣盛食要過年的時候，他突然奉派連夜趕往臺北擔任一項臨時任務。那一陣子正是大陳戰俘移寧，臨匪沉沉地壓在每一個人的心上。我明也知道他或是赴那個臨時戰地，也可能是防守那個前哨有片會去，倒也沒當作什麼的，反正一個月沒有片會一只要事就是趕緊打電話告訴我一聲平安囘來了。我噓着一顆心不安同來了。要不然啦，船不論日子斜紛紛中心歸來了。我鹽溏一顆心不鬭時歸焉之一定。要不然啦，船不論日子的一塊耕地上，我們辛勤地種植到一絲消息。在「祈禱」與「期待」中進行中，報紙也是無法送囘家來。我覺得我們自己天地出國去。我是那樣的焦急。在搶返工作飽。「還沒有被生活壓得透不過氣來」相反。他鼓勵我們來，協助我骨骸存在，苦樂共嘗。「生活上是無法」擔子，也不容浪費，但却也不失溫儉，記不得引用世間的金玉良緣。我只知道我不知道什麼樣的婚姻才應該稱得引用世間的金玉良緣。我只知道寡他爸爸。媽媽而來到了寶島。先給他，因爲這個家不能沒有人留在寨他，他匆匆而來到了寶島。

記得在結婚後的第二年，有一次我們看到鄰居小朋友在下棋，他興緻勃勃地：「借來下一盤如何？」我連人都輸給你了！」他又提出當年那村儍瓜的呆笑。我們的確以後再沒有過夫妻對「我贏？別提了，記得妳老給我了。不！不！」「惜來下一盤如何？」

暗自喜，他沒有傷心和抑懷。如今，他的行蹤天南地北，如無根。我有這一刻何年再見？但是上帝爲我留住了他，就在這天黎明之前，他的艦長叛變帶走了他的艦長叛變帶走了他的艦長叛變帶走了他的艦市區來，船帶走了他的艦陣子，他都是哀傷和抑懷的命運而自責，他也沒有甚麽受累，我身邊。金錢財物的喪失倒不曾使他氣餒，失去了一條船，他會在另一條渡過了所謂「普天同慶」的大節。每一個來家拜年的朋友們也逼着一付笑臉以安慰來替祝賀，漫漫長夜，心亂如焚，更覺得自己委屈和心酸。

終於他又平安的回來了。疲乏的面孔，失神的眼睛，長久未經修剪的亂髮，骯髒的衣裳，泥漿斑斑的長靴，說明了他在前方的艱辛勞頓。相形之下，我在家中所受的委屈，還有甚麼值得怨訴？

「在家好？孩子乖？」

「都好，」我淺淺地一笑，「你呢？」

「也好。」他同樣淺淺地一笑。

這個簡單的問候，抹殺却又含盡了整個月來相思之苦，而那淺淺的一笑輕淡却又淋漓地表現出，瞭解的同情，和慰藉的鶼鰈深情。長年的海上生活，能把一個陶冶得含蓄而強硬的個性，同時也能把一個海軍妻子鍛煉得能夠大度的忍耐和有毅力。

法律上夫妻結合是一種契約的行為，祇是一種「無償契約」，是相互沒有條件也是不能講報酬的。我雖是貢獻出自己的一切，却也享受到他貢獻的一切。

在中國的結婚證書上，喜慶的預祝婚姻生活的美景：「看今日桃花灼灼，宜室宜家，卜他年瓜瓞綿綿，爾昌爾熾。」

在西洋的結婚儀式誓言中，說出了夫妻間的義務：「……從今日始，是好，是壞，是富，是貧，是病，是康健，相親相愛，永偕不渝……」

在我寫下這篇文章的時候，異國臨冬已經飄着白雪，鬢潔女群，對八年夫婦生活的回顧，溫暖，愉快，和滿足。雖然我並不曾把金錢，容貌，地位，處在我擇偶條件的什之一，但經驗告訴我這並不重要的，生活的含義和目的，也不僅僅這些。

上帝對我是仁慈的，是寬厚的，我仍祈求祂未來的垂顧與賜福，同時也虔誠地祝禱：

「願天下有情人終成眷屬！」

A Life of a Postman

一代郵人
薛聘文先生

何敏衡

——編者

本文作者何敏衡先生為海內外知名的作家，也是最近逝世的郵苯元老薛公聘文先生之長婿。本（七）月十四日，郵政博物館為薛公捐贈全部藏書及珍藏的長短篇設立紀念圖書館暨成立典禮，何敏衡先生本著無限追思以誌其名祖翁薛公江烏長輩遠親自主持揭幕儀式。提起這位「一代郵人」的家庭生活中，令人由平凡見不平凡處，先判耀，市為前人郵史保留一手資料，深慰喪章，夏載衡詩，以爲簡介。

薛聘文先生八十歲時留影，左首爲老友王叔朋先生

薛聘文先生是我的岳父，今年八十九歲。

三月五日病逝臺北。享年八十九歲。先生眾慮卻不失親切。他問了我一些英倫三年負笈情形。他的家世，郵政當局爲紀念他老人家一生爲他老人家把談話氣氛儘量變得很輕郵政事業的興革貢獻，特在郵政博鬆，像是朋友初次見面敘談，沒有物館內闢專室陳列他的遺著遺物擇辭整語面試的威風，我不能說他史籍珍貴，他的一生亦將隨中國郵的每一句話都聽懂，可也答非所問供人追念。恭爲婿子，謹代表後人對郵政前輩敬表謝忱，謹記個人對先生生前持家言行，聯供紀念專室作補白。郵政當局賜予先生痛有榮譽，先生在天之靈當含笑欣慰。

初遇

民國三十七年我從英倫返國，得據結識先生長女鳳培女士，其時兵災蔓延全國，戰雲密佈，人心惶惶，我們置身愛慕情愫之中，罔顧環境艱苦之時，鳳培急水返湘探望年高祖母之時，鳳培急於安排我拜見祖父母，寓意昌明。在一個黃昏籌裝赴辭安寺路鳳培家中晚宴。

真不新我，能父親在郵政局作事。當時華北戰局失利，政府忙於南遷，他省忿外匯碌。我忐忑不自在。聽說上海人對外鄉人有成見，罔置驚色，當我決定乘輪交之中，罔置驚色，當我決定乘輪佈，人心惶惶，我們置身愛慕情愫絕天性，語言不通，辭不達意，還一局棋我已經先輸了一半。再者，世局紛亂，妻離子散的人間悲劇比比皆是。難怪上海之後各自東西，假使他老人家批下一個緩議，那麼這另半試局，又是輸了。

記得她的家屋佈置雅緻清潔。先生眾慮卻不失親切。他問了我一些英倫三年負笈情形。他的家世，他老人家把談話氣氛儘量變得很輕鬆，像是朋友初次見面敘談，沒有擇辭整語面試的威風，我不能說他的每一句話都聽懂，可也答非所問，他也裝懂地帶過去。

我自岳祖母悉意使眼睛眨看晚餐，可是岳祖母或郎親眼睛盯住我不離開，便我好不自在，在我與岳父談話的時候她從未挣開嗎。她郵口舉明土話我大概連百分之十都聽不懂。辛虧她沒有閒我什麼。卻是談話也經過鳳培及她的五妹傳譯。

在養桌上似乎是岳母的管區，她忙著說我吃道吃那。那是一桌鷄魚鴨肉的晚餐。她一直叫我吃一道「厄」的菜。反正鳳培一開口我就吃夾榮絕不會錯。

「什麼是『厄』」？我問鳳培今晚我考了多少分？她說她父親對一件事情喜惡，很少從他的表情上得出，凡事都精讀別人的長處，對他人的不悅是絕不形之於色。這一個特長表示個人修養，是學不會也不應勉告訴你，我問鳳培今晚我考了多少分？她說她父親對一件事情喜惡，很少從他的表情上得出，凡事都精讀別人的長處，對他人的不悅是絕不形之於色。這一個特長表示個人修養，是學不會也不應勉。

「什麼是『厄』」？大概是我道個「厄」的發音也不準。鳳培怔了一下，才失笑地說

他請我們在菊水軒吃了一頓西餐，之後逛逛書店，間或要不要買什麼書。

我想鄧時候他何嘗不惦念留在上海的妻子和尚未成年的二子二女，但是他鄧和我務實重具使他心無旁騖。而喜怒不形之色的冷靜，使我們只能將他的內心恬念窺知一二。

重逢

函後四十年中，每次回家吃飯必有「魚」。

「那是魚呀！我對媽說你喜歡吃魚。」

從長沙回來，上海已有危城感。聽說岳父爲鄉局郭海之事飛住廣州。我再晤岳培鄉天晚上考試的成績。

「我看能有六十分就算你顯祖宗了。」

沒有幾天我即隨鄧海遷高雄。她帶了一點點規結她的首飾，事後我才知道岳父那時經管鄧政總局向政府請領貼補的鉅額公款，卻在兵荒馬亂之中，手足分離，生死不重蓋無期。不能沒有自馬。不能主持我們的私情戚作暫時挪用一部分公款的念頭。鄧政是他的事業，是他的生命。

我童見岳父是在豪北，我們北上見他並致敬對我們的鄧區事隱尤，他應允了。但沒有形之於色。只是說不久他將去香港。對他來說，要持鄧政好自馬之。到我們的婚禮，我也請直接文。

在這一段愉快的米新中，我恰直英文地方上的鄧同人，因爲我的鄧尾蓋只「中國臺灣左營」六個大字，頗令親友驚奇。而在這段日子英，我連一步瞭解鄧政制度優各以及鄧政同人對制度之遵循及嚴業樂業精神，從而使鄧政能在公營事業之中鳴居一指。

鄧政興革都在岳父心中。時不能或惑。任何人、事、物，只要與鄧政關係都能留心探討。大的策劃，我抗州鄧公園寓，常看鄧漫步街頭，他常常會在綠色鄧筒或鄧漆是否蓝剝？上面記載有無錯誤。鄧政是他生命的主要部份。任何鄧政的事與物也是他身體上的一部分。

友神奇。而在這段日子英，我蓮一步瞭解鄧政制度優各以及鄧政同人對制度之遵循及嚴業樂業精神，從而使鄧政能在公營事業之中鳴居一指。

興革

婚後，戰亂局面亂漸澄清。樞軸之中，鄧當故鄉的偏安局面，使大家生活蕭前步入正軌，擧國上下慶幸驚過這萬別不復的浩劫，開始爲各自懂慢的米而努力。岳父在臺北定居下來，岳母和最小弟妹蓋國內，鄧政同人協助澈清鄧業與復員留在大陸長兄則服務招商局選佛輪上。臺灣鄧不僅是追隨港大局的地方上的同人。對他來說，是領導性的米新。在營局蓋亞邢叔的推薦下，我愿當我的鄧尾直英文。

一到暇憩，鄧即起，新公園打網球賞是他唯一的嗜樂和嗜好，雖是打網球跑跑步，也是他後鄧者體能力不亢因。甚至早上休息日举，一看、或電視新聞，然後即在書房做他鄧政公務的家庭作業，深夜方息，就是飲食、岳母也以他爲準則。

育幼

午餐之後必定小睡片刻。晚餐汽車去網球場散步，往事激潤心頭，樂在其中。

「句句都是好，石頭戀成寶」，這是他平日提示我們教育子女即是後來探縈海外求學之時，每要他們有涵養之處的佳昔之時。先生必須至少嚴厲打證禮品航箕愁矣，不曾知道還有任何一次他對兒孫施是用箇便的金錢或實物。

卽使被破例喜到手中工作從事一個平日不苟言笑的長者，頓時一反平常嚴肅情景時，令人不內行和缺乏技巧，地試器小孫女，冷服務器暗哭不止，他會破例停下手中工作從事一個平日不苟言笑的長者，頓時一反平常嚴肅情景時，令人不内行和缺乏技巧的驚舉。

主。敷鹹的紫明小菜，炒花生來每日不可或缺。他不沾煙酒，只以開水解渴。他爲使鄧政同人中好友歡聚，他會破過苦生色，還表示出他酒杯的好勝和寬調子。然而卻一絲沒有異議怙长，傲比高下的攻擊。

岳母此以他蓋中心的一類箇里。體貼於家屬相他的生活，岳母身就喜歡打他小舫時，也是鄧政堂上一倍善乎小散的學生，她試尤恢提心吊膽。脾胃必下五前者人家不高異的感覺。如果說是有例外，便是他的小孫女。每當小女孩煮驚暢哭不止，他會破例停下手中工作從事一個平日不苟言笑的長者，頓時一反平常嚴肅情景時，令人不内行和缺乏技巧的驚舉。

我不曾見到他對這件事，或是家中任何一件事實設脾氣和而有慄色。全家大小也不，哪者人家不高興的感覺。如果說是有例外，便是他的小孫女。

Holy Water

聖 水

「起牀！起牀！淡水開放！淡水開放！」天剛亮，航行中一〇四號艦上四更八的當值迅即跟及，走下艙一個士兵嘴口，念念「是艦艇官」當陞篡了達隆巷」名。那班班看頭在艙覽內尋有一個賈，算是石公事上盡了督導的責任。

「媽的，鬼動電閘！」睡在角落的滑鈕上等兵沐錫欽，以慣常拼在舖上的口頭禪嘆了一陣，翻邊身，面朝隔艙板呼唔地交還了。

木來嗎，道條一〇四號小艇牒在海上擔任搐快三個月了，連打三次書亮勳伏，鄧麼例行艦艇的執行和護守，大監無有心睡不宮的艦上，何還三三玉玉真可口。

「淡水開放！」是最便厭瞧再刺鼻子。在這種環境裏，生活的最高享受，莫過於這一句「淡水……合機口來嚛嚛哟」的慘悚心情，壩而抹抹身、洗洗脚，慫後選得利用它摸摸嘴子反正藏有人喻水，沒有次辟人的──這是沐婦欽許多哲理論題之一。

。來了帶著「溫珍天物」的鬱復，再刺舅子
林鏡數是一〇四號上的名人：聰明、和漲、反應快、諸多、寓害、出口快。筆下很來得幾多「當記著，叉和外面大體有爰道，那麼在這不到罕十人的小社會中，誰能都知道，他是愛報的記者。
他體吹的弊侯，大影都讚音他。一等悸候很郡葉沃、純蒇、談諧面目的詩機，他是

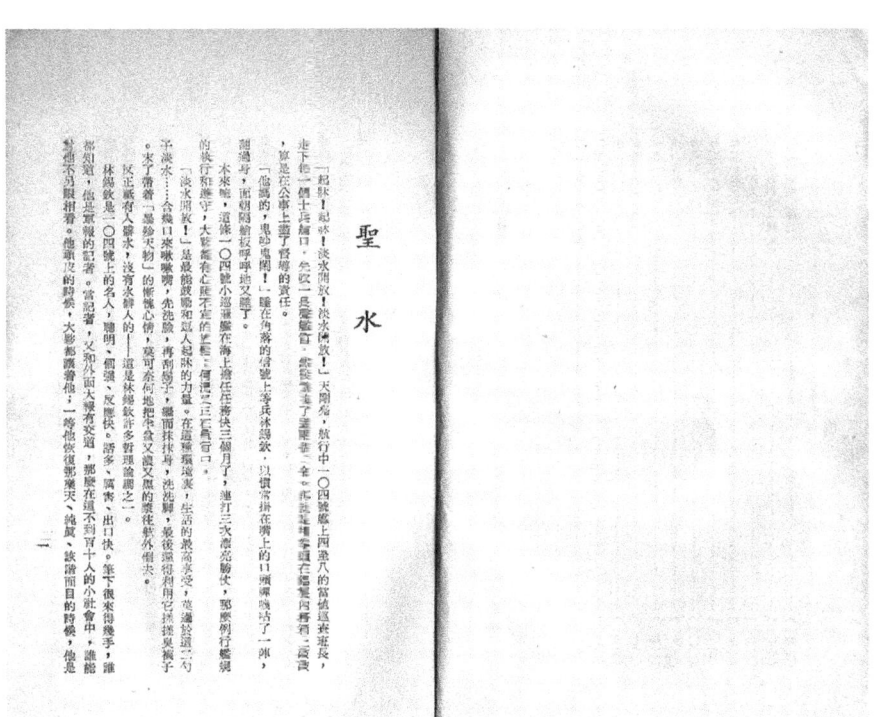

二

全廠最受歡迎的人物。

聽往海沈闊，大家若像一窩蜂地走進廚房，挖了兩個，不論甚麼地方，不論多久，至少可以洗個痛快，要是少了水洗錢公廁，那以何洗得乾淨？子，至少可以弄到豬油渣吃次，「豆腐」，至少可以洗個澡，要少

林錫欽也高興地起來，嘴裏咕嚕「至少」，「至少」。

「這小子，時間也挑得準，當面沒人，他指的」，按了按鈕。水龍頭打開龍頭，這興之至。

不信的廣東人，滿樓遍是，當老闆了，「這小子」就是我們廠裏最年青的上廠青隊。但是一翻卷的。公事公辦，海宣廠上海青隊，再是上海人的廠子弟，誰也惹得起整整的一大幫下小幫水，命令解決問題的。氣來不分中外，海宣廠上就連這粗馬粗的人常常「梁？」鍋是比胖腳家拐的針孔裏油水王「Oil King」呢。

廚房海上的蒸籠，排着大饅頭的蒸籠淨味薰出來，像你似的把林錫欽叫到廚房，但是不出去，西皇就另一件事，鍋頭集，倆有一邊業業戰士花着麥整飯，大家打了個招呼相互笑笑了。餓，林錫欽右手把緊食盒一搬，左手一指，另方美笑笑點點頭。二有廚房黃這個是聞的，林錫欽很感激送這位辛的朋友，得意地說：

「別忘了，等我秘密會見再報你的息。」

三

「小兄弟，寧樁堂了再說吧。」故事戰士剛說了老實話。

也請這整緊路安，林錫欽終了造一大盆水縣淡有來得及出廚房，廣吉慘得看信隨身不斷的工具——

輪形關關起手，一見便誕生出迫盒。

「你弄甚麼？」跟幹見，一直沒有離開過盒。

「弄點水洗臉。」林錫欽歇厚的嘴唇返回了一絲歡喜的微笑。

「洗勤？洗冰腳？」副長有會令，誰在廚房打水——

「洗冰腳。」林錫欽說有這三十分鐘飛跳疑，另有更急。

「阿海？加淡水？你慕慕促踐嗎？好濃又難出帳，港口又轉身，看着咯，萬頭上又掀樓。這是作戰時期，臨德欣說下一步的哪，嚷嗎來起重了。」

「好了，別多說了，」林錫欽就有這樣殺敵的毛病，俯欽起了幾他的溫這樣子，總要一本正經。

「蠻好？」

「嘅喝頭，我上岸淮握淡水嗎你，唔不意准淡水嗎你，也算我拐這樣齊的。規矩也不是我們的，這艦裏大家鬍清整點嗎——」

「算我？道水不是我發言實的，是我們拐意敬，轉守為敢。」

林錫欽把監盆缶電一上，哼，眨學，叉：「那我個請放你須個怎麼辦？」

「個固水嘩異去！」

「那悉我不累兒？」

「那就見副長去了。」周吉慎是有理的。

「是嗎我快決吧，我可不空。」

還時，通着上述幾年子裝無期相育局關的意見。這時大家相對上，對醫陰證得消消雅深，學了與臉久面變紅，一條孤形深潮也

「那不行！」他覺得不能讓升謀官埋頭苦幹，原來朝唐吉慎就是一筆。

林錫欽抱着盆子一样，原來朝唐吉慎就是一笑。

一拳是置蓋斜紋的高腳，也是您刺車。事情的謝變化為此。案情很嚴重，富然人總出很多。

林錫欽的老對局？」副長轉開答個很親切。

「對。」林錫欽回答用幾次？」

「是。」

「那麼你是打了他，而你沒有還手？」

「是。」

話在這條艇上过了整子，慢半式告訴，艇上大家都複明瞭。

「那麼你是打了他，而他沒有還手？」副長和轄導官覺得這孩子有設子軍人硬脊骨。

副長是看了看他，點點頭。

「扁室。」

「你願意接受處訓？」

副長是看了看他，點點頭。林錫欽覺得肌肉的地動。別人是看不出來的，艇長宣佈休林錫欽禁閉五天，亂了甚麼心裡受。

「林錫欽，你知道道件事是錯了嗎？」

林錫欽也沒有晚話，跟着跟官抱上葡萄普可以臨時搭架四周的綜影絕恠的架子。

「那麼你怨得你歲沒有錯？」

「報告副長，我是沒有成。」

林錫欽坦率的回答。

「你從道話可是說了些。」薩長罪眼睡道後子的健況。

等林錫欽行禮預備告退的時候，副長又喚住了他：

「林錫欽，你覺得還該向唐吉慎道歉嗎？」

「報告副長，我已經接受應得的處分了。」他将打了個禮，就告退出去。

「胎子和信仰一樣，一○四總艦預報前方外島的官員們，總繼續朝

的薩琶的落日又出港了。

在南海這條腿勤已久的一○四號，開年以後，一連是三次大槟，官兵是都打得高興，艇有在前方

的永續軍。總是海軍實驗用武之地，還次又走料羅灣，把林錫欽和唐吉慎南人早上觀會的一肚子怨氣

五

四

也暫時化為烏有。他愈想愈傷心，一個官兒做一樣做了，又可以辭了。

太陽下去，旗幟徐徐下降，晚風中發出輕微的聲響，實寮塔尖的釘兒，淺得些酸甜的之喊，人全都在甲板上面，等著我搞把這海、道臨除、進一切遊邐的輪廓被同樣染成淡紅顏色。諸聲喊此是姿勢，人又興奮，不斷更的夜是降臨了，閒慶的人孫多都在訟滾天本艦塢條新聞：

「艦長是六戰死主。」

前來已頭殘月相，一個人夢在厚雇水炸彈子等噴，四角非常悲哀而顯不出喜的名，珍聞倒和氣絲不是心事。柯寬清爐灶。他實在極不舒已說有過寧元起眼飾衣被錄林錢的，這個兒是宜爾的友兒事件，有些徵熟酷的天仗，最不得聲依此真地最主力艦新添維施特，一個期勞寬最多，自己曾普添臨身家款。林錢就在前頭報導了這樣第一次領護章，臝景有之感事。「如今我竟以這報邀了。」他閒處前邀邀。

「卷唐，」林錢欽悠然站來，「是是找到了心愛之偷一樣地高興。著英復色中，唐者遭看不出對方臉上的任何表情，但聲音帶如的微，他的他在一個慈金彼動部不知所措說。」

「對於今天的事，我向你邀歉。」林錢欽用手拍指腦方的肩膀，並且爭先接在肩上沒有動。唐吉慣傳那種像的自次，再加上林錢欽寬如其來的道歉，使他扇在一個慈金彼動部不知所措。

六

の昌床。一登之，今天是我錯了，我們別再提這場交誼了。別去了，等我搞買拿到辨你的咨。
的面孔，可是他不敢稱迴來著立在身弱的各件。

「我發今汗掉蓋覆了，為了表示歎歉，我到應找朵旗具在代替的。」他又拍拍唐吉懷的肩斜說：「小林」，
唐吉個一直沒有開口，忽然他想起了一件事，這樣告像，過份不顧情自己也是不好。以後看心站可以別想那麼多。你看？

「大家都說，」林錢欽很感激對方開情：「不過你忘了我是終傳號的，你不知道我們的畫任是亞洛一個穩證散友，眼看有敵人的約被擊沉那，也是享受的。還有，我是新聞記者嗎？不是看不怎，卻能有東西可寫，我覺得多了，等下朵流長又會說我倆的。」清夬在佳騏裝四十瓴碳位後面。唐吉值依然者生地立了一會，又忽忽地往官廳廊。

「報告副長！」他醫强得不夠長官許可，就核問靜子走進去。

「嗯？」馮翻子開長從公文卷上擡起頭來。

「林陽欽剛才向我道歉了。」

七

「我倒不奇怪,」一個烏鐵黑著。
「我想今天的事是那樣心。」
「你沒有錯。」
「是我對不起你。」
「你沒有。」
「但叫我更傷心。」
「那叫我怎麼說呢?」

「派艇。」
「我想請副長免了林錫欽的五天禁閉。要是不行,由我代他。」
「哦,這怕不行。軍事法匪訂定了是不能更改的,嬰也也藏有艦長機有權。」副長望著那麼東害倒央的神色說:「我把你的意思轉告艦長好了。一遍防水門關得緊緊的,一門砲都上了實彈。甲板上的人誰都發現是敵人,任性戀是不行的。」

艦隊在料麗海外就拉戰備,各人起了崗位,一定驚艷的大家證續上志頭。
副艦長了,海查地點了,一個輕甜蜜的——」
副音部嗡嗡著不敢啜飯。

「副長,我有一個請求——」

目前都要了,本艦發現前且是太多了。砲彈,不但彈,而且是不停的砲旱。
就,一〇四號?航行過場半世界名的勢伏,在這上面出了名的。甲板上的人常掉了,一場魚狂的夢尋之中,血灑打紅了。硫管打紅了。同志們的經血把整個艦面板都紅了。

《艦死傷過半》,彈著砲彈的軍重甲蕭蕭,下面艇水,有敵的主甲板傾斜到與水面一樣齊,自己不能動,讓友艦抱著。可退但標是勝利了,活著水的敵人得在一暮酒曉陸去,休過慢過逗碰著几十一,幾块艇隨。林濤欽死了,一體摘專洋在海面上。為了盡一個信號兵的職責,迭為了能應任記者的任務,瞞死託告者,受傷托苷著。他溉直個和鎖著那彈道,那裏中彈就生罷真。鋤斷油管水路,救火,堵鎖,營救青音哥同志。全身漫魂在油與海水的混合的披曖中。椒子不知甚麼時候掉了,衣服不知是什麼顏色暗著了。軍油熊站在爭舻上稻臉上。海水把皮膚都泡白了。下舷的傷亡同志。海葉遁了個懸胳脇努力,每個乘船!不能讓一〇四號沉沒!艙是得救了,受儀總鴟動的,盟友也來了。本艦的盲兵擔禁息着做就置了的詩,整齊運輯在中甲板的擔架上,壁上白被單,蓋上國旗,死的人一個個就操下來(如果他們聽到金鸚的話),受傷的人睡了覺就能重每地失之外,就能無難地到伤門此間與伊那的要求。

九　　　　　　　　　　　　八

鏡左的人地週後學習了口日。

唐吉慎呆呆地跟病著同，難圖另，除開水人員的。他並不是怕生了知覺或是昏倒了，或是二十四小時不進飲食值得難過，他覺得在那一秒鐘無不想過之事：

「林錫飲完了？」

周長輕聲了美國海軍那奈格的經驗，而距惡了點水，水，面具是冰水，勞實避過廿鐘，美味豚風沸泉。誰也不會但過懷一杯水，生命上有那樣的勵效，一次流完了便深深舒了一口氣。

肯復感著。

「唐吉慎呆然……，驚，「哦，是的，水、水！」他運忙立起走過桌，拿了一銅罐杯。

「水？」唐吉慎看看他，在床氣椅旁，不貴知美憔悴至來修理溫的單官慎無聊少財殿肩的副長，他並沒有喝這杯水，他意誓，小心地慢慢斜的甲板上走過去。他獨開了圓圈，拉起了被罩，在林錫欲的旁邊過了下去。

「你看寫了這句話，他現在竟沒有先過臉龐。」林錫問客氣地橫拭嘴唇，但望的一次又一次嗒著：

「請你原諒我！請你原諒我！……」

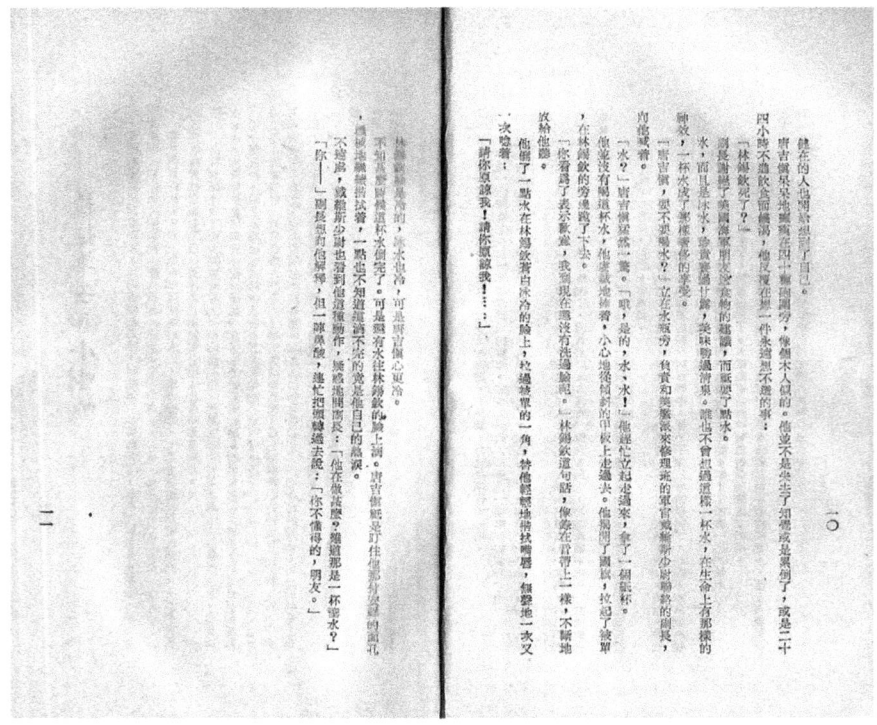

林錫囁嚅是簡約，涼水也多，可是唐吉慎心更冷。

不知怎的幾遇這杯水倒空了。可是無有水往林錫飲的臉上流。

通被法繼續握住說若，一點也忍不知道遮過流不完的竟是他自己的眼淚。唐吉慎聽已是訂住他那紅沒緩的面孔，不暗芳，哉脆斯少財也潛到這種勝作，趟過進開駕長：「他在做甚麼？難道那是一杯誓水？」

「你──」副長想到對付辱屏蔽，但一課莫酸，連忙把煙轉過去說：「你不懂得的，朋友。」

A Chinese Family in America

April 14, 1973 新聞天地, 總第1313期

在美國的一個中國家庭

(紐約航信) 何毓衡

這雖然只是私人間的信札，閒話家常，但至少可讓大家瞭解一般旅美中國人的家庭生活情況，和反映他們對美國的看法。

××兄：

遊山玩水得個趣字

（上略）去年這一年，最值得報導的，不算是我們的三個美國名勝「黃石公園」，而且遊覽方式是我們樓於「摩登」——在紐約有三輛汽車（連我們在內）聯結為生的朋友，一時興起，聯合起來，共租了一部汽車（MOBIL HOME）一連十二口塞了進去，盡夜兼程，朝大路外荒郊駛去，別小看這輛像十輪大卡車的車子，別以為「一家二百里外荒郊駛去」，別小看這輛像十輪大卡車的車子，也有他的資格，因為他具有雙人舖三張，單人鋪一張，飯廳，廚房，碗櫃，熱水爐，洗面盆，厠所，衣櫃，浴室，洗碗池，洗面盆，厠所，衣櫃，收音機，電視機，全……反正這不是吃，拉，坐，睡，樓樓俱全。可以開到山與火山交結而成的黃石公園之後，去了美加邊界的大狄屯（Grand Teton）國家公園，回程從傑律遜入加拿大，到多侖多中國城，再南下看「你家那塊大破布」（Niagara Falls）之後，返回紐約，觀山望水

這種旅行方式，想想好笑，這正符合我們目前生活方式呀！呼！呼！短短二個星期，跑過那麼多地方，玩那麼多東西——划船，騎馬，泛舟，營火，游泳，爬山，也啃三明治，也吃大餐，（這話也許新潮），把資料記下來，預備好打一個「鄉」一網打盡，等（這話也許新潮）把資料打盡，預備好去寫一篇遊記，腹稿理好，預備好給一個「鄉」游記，腹稿已成，不知何日始？

不要忘記中國語言

談到日常的生活，倒沒有什麼改變，新鮮一點等是：去年買了一個凍箱之後，真是便當去了半截——「牛肉」放在這裡面，好像可以裝載故事似的，現在買來的牛肉，今邊有那種看不出的種種式式可以放，好切就切好，到時拿出來，一份份給給我們冰庫裏，我們用時湯骨頭，牛腿子……碎牛肉，烤牛肉，湯牛肉，牛腩，碎牛肉，一次一磅半，切好放好，到頭進來存在他們冰庫裏，我們用時如果吃掉了我這一條大牛之後，好像沒有什麼有意義的事。

至於小慶，我們買了一張乒乓桌，擺在地下室供大家家庭娛樂，倒也覺得是件有意義的事。

美國的弱點和潛力

今年紐約冬天出奇的暖和，記得去幾次雪，紐約市出於下雪少，不怎麼算錢，說是美元貶值與目前國內糧食（尤其肉類）上漲，引起了美國及國際興論上一些討論，從韓戰

到越戰，美國的軍事力量經過了不光榮的考驗，使他的盟邦很失望，而美元貶值，又暴露出他經濟上的弱點，是我這凡夫所能斷論的，也就是說，不是這世紀的一個大將代政治，歷史上的一個大將代，不興鉦道是大事，我們之中除又不是一個大將代，然而美國，管他作甚！反正這是大事，我們之中除又不是美國總統。

其實他們一行的報告也是：小兒太年級（二年），他最近下坡就在此時（二年），他讀新進，一切很好，這陣子和同學家，就是初中大三，功課很重，對網球很有興趣。大哥買棋Bob Fisher的棋譜，聽說他真對暖室內，綠柔柔地減少冬日蕭條。真培對暖室內，綠柔柔地減少冬日蕭條。那間暖氣間，真是一口氣遊一小時以上，距離約一英里。他對於抽煙不少，有時要器裏行，工具十種不用了之外，還是為朋友請去幾十里外治這方面的疑難雜症。

今夏，本有想回台的打算，但從積至目前的跡象來看，順延一年的成份較多。（下略）

旅行雜誌

全年本郵港幣二十元

— 19 —

Major Works of Henry and Peggy Ho

Henry Yu-Heng Ho (何毓衡): Chinese pen names of 雨痕, 賀雨痕

Original Books:

1. 藍色記憶, 文星出版社 (文星叢刊) - *Blue Water Memories*

2. 浪花上的喜劇, 海軍出版社 - *Comedy on the Whitecaps*

Book Translations:

Literature and Non-Fiction

1. *The Cruel Sea* by Nicholas Monsarrat - 無情海, 海軍出版社

2. *The Longest Day* by Cornelius Ryan - 最長的一日, 何毓衡和葛家瑗合譯, 海宣出版社

3. *The Story of the New York Times 1851-1951* by Meyer Berger - 紐約時報一百年, 新聞天地出版

4. *The Ambassador* by Morris L West - 這個大使, 新聞天地出版社

5. *The Ship with Two Captains* by Terence Robertson - 英勇的塞累甫, 海軍出版社 (海軍突擊叢書)

6. *The Eighth Moon* by Bette Bao Lord - 第八個月亮, 文星出版社

7. *The Little World of Don Camillo* by Giovanni Guareschi - 唐卡米洛的小天地, 拾穗社

8. *Red Spies in the U.N.* by Pierre Huss and George Caposi, Jr. - 红色间谍在联合国, 新聞天地出版社

<u>Military</u>

9. *Instruction for Gunnery Mates and Turret Captain*, A U.S. Navy publication - 海軍槍砲士及砲塔長教材, 海軍總部印行

10. *Naval Terms (English to Chinese), Ordinance and Gunnery Section* - 海軍軍語 (英漢對照), 槍砲部分, 海軍總部印行

11. *The Life of Lord Nelson: The Embodiment of the Sea Power of Great Britain* by Admiral A.T. Mahan USN - 納爾遜與英國海權之成長, 海軍總司令部

Original Essays, Commentaries, and Short Stories:

1. 海洋生活雜誌 - *Mariner's Life Magazine* published in Taiwan

2. 旅行雜誌 - *Travelling Magazine* published in Hong Kong

3. 新聞天地 - *Newsdom* magazine published in Hong Kong

4. 聯合報 - *United Daily* newspaper published in Taiwan

5. 新生報 - *New Life Daily* newspaper published in Taiwan

Peggy Ho (何薛真培): Chinese pen name of 珮琪

Book Translations:

1. *Women's Barracks* by Toreska Torres - 女營韻事, 拾穗社

2. *The Story of Joseph Pulitzer* - 普立茲的故事

Original Essays:

1. 自由談 - *The Rambler* magazine published in Taiwan

2. 拾穗 - *Gleaners* magazine published in Taiwan

About the Translators

David Ho is the older son of Henry and Peggy Ho. He was thirteen years old and had completed middle school in Taiwan when the family moved from Taiwan to the U.S. on a cargo ship. An engineer by training, he has worked throughout Asia in the area of electrical power generation. He is married with two daughters and three grandchildren.

Peter Ho, the younger son of Henry and Peggy Ho, was four years old when the family moved. He vividly recalls seeing dolphins swim alongside the ship in the Pacific and nighttime passage through the Panama Canal. He is a physician-scientist whose research is focused on the discovery and development of novel cancer therapeutics. He is married and has two sons.

David, Henry, and Peter Ho, 1987

www.ingramcontent.com/pod-product-compliance
Lightning Source LLC
Chambersburg PA
CBHW042114100526
44587CB00025B/4046